NORSE MYTHOLOGY FOR KIDS

Legendary Stories, Quests & Timeless Tales From Norse Folklore. The Myths, Sagas & Epics of The Gods, Immortals, Magic Creatures, Vikings & More

History Brought Alive

© Copyright 2021 - All rights reserved.

The content contained within this book may not be reproduced, duplicated or transmitted without direct written permission from the author or the publisher.

Under no circumstances will any blame or legal responsibility be held against the publisher, or author, for any damages, reparation, or monetary loss due to the information contained within this book, either directly or indirectly.

Legal Notice:

This book is copyright protected. It is only for personal use. You cannot amend, distribute, sell, use, quote or paraphrase any part, or the content within this book, without the consent of the author or publisher.

Disclaimer Notice:

Please note the information contained within this document is for educational and entertainment purposes only. All effort has been executed to present accurate, up to date, reliable, complete information. No warranties of any kind are declared or implied. Readers acknowledge that the author is not engaged in the rendering of legal, financial, medical or professional advice. The content within this book has been derived from various sources. Please consult a licensed professional before attempting any techniques outlined in this book.

By reading this document, the reader agrees that under no circumstances is the author responsible for any losses, direct or indirect, that are incurred as a result of the use of the information contained within this document, including, but not limited to, errors, omissions, or inaccuracies.

FREE BONUS FROM HBA: EBOOK BUNDLE

Greetings!

First of all, thank you for reading our books. As fellow passionate readers of history and mythology we aim to create the very best books for our readers.

Now, we invite you to join our VIP list. As a welcome gift we offer the History & Mythology Ebook Bundle below for free. Plus you can be the first to receive new books and exclusives! Remember it's 100% free to join.

Simply click the link below to join.

Click Here For Your Free Bonus

(https://www.subscribepage.com/hba)

Keep upto date with us on:

YouTube: History Brought Alive

Facebook: History Brought Alive

www.historybroughtalive.com

TABLE OF CONTENTS

Introduction
    History Brought Alive
        Citations

Chapter 1: What Are Myths
    Types of Myths
        The Gods
        The Creation of Humans
        Human Behavior and Emotions
        Heroes
        Where Do Myths Come From?

Chapter 2: Who Were The Norse
    The Norse Myths
        How It All Began
        Ymir, His Sweaty Kids, and A Cowlick
        The Gods of the Aesir Age
        The World is Like a Body
        The Sun, The Moon, The Stars, And The End

Chapter 3: The Nine Worlds
    The World Tree Is Also Named Yggdrasil
        Five Plus Four Worlds Sitting In A Tree
        Asgard: The Place the Aesir Call Home
        Vanaheim: Home of the Vanir
        Alfheim: Where the Pretty Elves Live

Niflheim: Ice Here, Ice There, Ice Ice Everywhere

Chapter 4: More About The Worlds of The World Tree

Muspel: It's on FIRE

Midgard: The Human Home

Jotunheim: A Gigantic Home

Svartalfheim: The Home Under the Ground

Helheim: Where the dead go on living

Other Facts About The World Tree

The Norns

The Numbers Game

Chapter 5: Humans, Gods, and Monsters

Creation of Humans

Where Bad Poets Come From

Chapter 6: Godly Adventures

Odin is Stuck to The Tree

Mimir Loses His Head

Chapter 7: More Godly Adventures

The Other God Of Poetry

How Loki Built a Wall and Odin Got a Spider Horse

Chapter 8: The Other Two Strongest Gods

Why Thor Gets Headaches

How Frey Got a Stag's Head

Chapter 9: Nine Mothers For Heimdall

Half Rig, Half Heimdall

Chapter 10: The End, or Is It?

The End is The Beginning is The End

Conclusion

Free Bonus from HBA: Ebook Bundle

References

INTRODUCTION

(Or, the part of the book no one reads unless they're your parents and they want you to fall asleep quickly.)

If you're the one reading this part, well then HELLO! It's very nice to meet you and tell you what this book is all about. We're sure you're thinking, "What do you mean, 'what the book is about'? Doesn't the title say 'Norse Mythology?'"

You're absolutely right! It is indeed. But we're also going to explore what the words *Norse* and *Mythology* actually mean, and then we'll take a closer look at the myths themselves. Did you know a lot of the Norse myths have also been talked about by other people in different ways? I'm sure you've heard the name Thor, especially with all the superhero movies that came out a few years ago. In this book, we'll tell you all about how Thor was born, how he grew up, and the things he did. Before all that, we'll also take a quick look at what myths are, where they come from, and why they're important. There are many, many reasons why they're important, but the main reason is because they are wonderful stories which people have loved for hundreds and thousands of years.

Yes, the stories are *that* old. Now, clearly they weren't written in English at first, and when someone decided to translate it into English, they used a very old and very difficult kind of English. But then, some people translated that story from English into their own language and some parts of the story changed! Have you heard the Cinderella story? Well, did you know the Egyptians (Climo & Heller, 1992), the Persians (Climo & Florczak, 2001), the

Native Americans (San, 1997) among many others have their own version of the story?

This is what happens when stories evolve. *Evolve* means when you change from what you were to something better. You might have heard in school that monkeys evolved into human beings. In the same way, stories evolved into monkeys — I mean myths!

These myths exist in every corner of the world, even the parts we haven't really explored. There were so many of them that slowly people decided these stories ought to be studied, so that others who want to learn about them will be able to understand them. Like you!

Perhaps once you've grown up, you will decide you want to study the myths properly and will read all those very grown up books such as *The Eddas* or *The Odyssey*. When you begin to study all of this you will discover how the word *myth* comes from the Greek word *Mythos*, which means tales, or story. Then perhaps you will love all the stories you read so much that you will decide to write your own story. And when you do, I know it will be utterly, and truly, excellent.

HISTORY BROUGHT ALIVE

At History Brought Alive we love learning about things that happened in the past. Even the not-so-nice parts. Which is why, the books we write will invite you to learn about the past in a fun way, and also remind you that the not-so-nice bits are just as important as the nice. We hope you will like what we write and how we write, so that you will read the books first, grow curious and read other books, and maybe one day go on to write books like these yourself! As you read through this book, we especially hope you like our book so much that you make a friend for life.

CITATIONS

When you read through the books, you might find some sentences ending with a name and a date, like so: (Orel, 2003). This means that someone else said the thing you read, long before anyone else. Imagine your friend told you a joke they came up with, but it was so good that you absolutely had to tell someone else. So, you do, but you also tell them that your friend told you the joke first, so that they don't think you came up with it or copied it from somewhere else.

We do this when writing as well. We look at something someone else has written, and we think it is so wonderful, we decide to put it into our stories, but we add the name and date at the end, so people will know we got it from someone else who is very good at writing, too. This is called giving someone *credit*.

It also means that if you want to read that person's stories, you can go to the end of this book, check the list of related books and websites, and use the name and date to see where the person said it. Then, you can get their book to read what they wrote and have an extra book to read!

CHAPTER 1: WHAT ARE MYTHS

When you think about the stories you like, which one is your favorite? I'll start. My favorite story is about King Arthur and all his knights, and all the adventures they went on. Perhaps you've read about it. According to the people of Britain, he was the greatest and most noble King who ever lived. And his friend, the wizard named Merlin, was the smartest wizard ever.

How do I know all of this? Well, because I read the story. But, how do I know if it's a true story or not? I don't. However, the people who study history for a living — they're called historians — have studied very old books, some written in 500 A.D and others around 1066 A.D. They realized that although all the other stuff about the wars and things might be true, they still have no proof that a king named Arthur existed (Staff, 2018). So why do people continue to believe these stories are true?

Well, because these stories gave people hope. A lot of the time, people's lives were very difficult, so to cheer each other up, they would tell each other it would be okay. But who would make it okay? How would things like war and sickness ever go away? So, people looked up at the sky when there was a storm and decided the thunder meant there was something or someone up there who was angry. When lightning flashed and someone in the fields got struck by it, they decided that that person must have done something wrong and that's why this happened. On the other hand, when someone fell ill, the person taking care of them must've thought, "Oh, if only someone could make my sister better." Then, a few days later when their sister became well without medicine, they must've thought, "Oh! There was a ray of sunlight in her room that day; maybe there was something magic in it!" And from there they would have talked it over with their friends and those people would have talked about it to others and this way the story would have spread among a whole village.

It was something to pass along to new generations so that they wouldn't forget. Some believed it, and some believed it wasn't true. Those who didn't, preferred to forget it as quickly and as easily as they could. Some people who believed it, decided to write it down and as more and more people decided it must be true because they believed it, it became an official myth or a religion.

TYPES OF MYTHS

Sometimes the kinds of myths that people told each other were all about how the world was created. But because most of the people in a country such as India had probably never seen a country like Iceland, they would not be able to imagine why people would need stories about a god of ice. But they would both agree when talking about a god or goddess of summer.

Not all of the myths were happy stories. Some were tragic, some were happy-ever-afters, and some were hilarious. But the one thing they had in common, was that the entire world had them.

THE GODS

It's difficult to know for certain whether the gods were created from the myths or whether the stories came after the gods. It's a little like the old question, 'Who came first, the chicken or the egg?'. Gods and myths are like the chicken and the egg question, but perhaps you shouldn't call a god "chicken head" to their face.

Did you know they made myths from that question too? The Greeks have a god named Alectryon (Alec-tree-un) who got turned into a rooster for falling asleep while he was supposed to be on guard (*Alectryon (mythology)*, 2021). But in Hindu mythology, a god named Brahma (Bruhm-ah) hatched from a golden egg and then created everything else (Cartwright, 2015).

The gods were said to control everything - from how humans behaved, to when the seasons changed, to how calm the sea was, how hard the wind blew, and even when you sneezed!

They almost always had families, and just like all families, they had good times and bad times. The bad news was, when they fought with each other, it was the humans they decided to mess with. Unfair, right?

If they're going to fight, they should keep it among themselves, don't you think? But because (according to the stories) they created the humans, they thought they had a right to treat us any way they wanted. If they were happy, they would be nice to humans; if they were annoyed, things could go very, very bad. And because they were immortal, their fights weren't the kinds of fights they would forget about — because they would stay alive forever, they would remember what the fight had been about and then they would either involve the humans, hold a grudge, or throw a temper tantrum that would end with a human dying.

THE CREATION OF HUMANS

After creating the world and everything else in it, the gods became bored. In their boredom, they decided to create humans. I mean, when I'm bored, I just read a book, but gods don't generally do that. I'm not sure if it's because they didn't have libraries or because they didn't think to invent books at that time. Anyway...

When they created humans, they decided to make them just like themselves, but without the immortality and special powers. Which, if I were among the first humans, I would be mad about this and demand to be remade properly with all sorts of powers and everything! Maybe I'd ask for the power to fly. What would you ask for?

The first humans didn't ask for anything of the sort. Some of them even lived in the cold and dark, shivering and afraid until one of the gods felt sorry for them and decided to make them a fire so they would have some light and warmth. I suppose the first humans were just so happy to be made, they did not think of it like that.

After doing this, the gods also gave the humans a bunch of dos and don'ts which they themselves did not follow — this is called hypocrisy (hip-pok-kruh-see). Hypocrisy is basically when someone who gives you rules or advice doesn't do the same. If you've ever heard the phrase, "Do as I say, not as I do," that counts as a form of hypocrisy! But alas, they were gods and they had all the power, so they weren't too bothered by it.

HUMAN BEHAVIOR AND EMOTIONS

Hidden in the stories we tell ourselves, and all the ones we repeat endlessly and over and over again, are also ideas which ease our pain and sadness. Now we know that our brain is what does this, but did you know that scientists have studied the brain and discovered that stories can make us change what our brains feel (Zak, 2013)? How it works is like this: our brains tell us that emotions are important because they create our motivations. This, in turn, pushes us to take action.

Think of it this way. Imagine you see a little duck on your way to school. When you come back home, you think the duck has gone home. The next day during breakfast, your mum reads a story from the newspaper about how the pond in your city has so much garbage in it that the ducks can't live in it any more. Your brain reminds you of the duck you saw and the story your mum just told makes you think of how sad the duck must feel.

Because of this story, you feel the duck's sadness, so you decide to do something about it. You tell your friends and your family, and all of you gather to slowly clean up the pond. Little by little, news about what you're doing spreads and everyone comes to help. Soon, the pond is clean again, and the ducks come back to the pond.

All of this happened because you understood how sad the duck must be feeling, and because you also took action. This is called empathy. Empathy is when you understand another person's emotions and you try to make it better.

In mythology, when gods have empathy for humans, nice

things happen. But more often than not, the gods are in bad moods. So, to try and help improve a god's bad mood so that humans wouldn't suffer, some humans would go on a quest, in the same way you would have for the duck – which would make you a duck hero!

HEROES

Some of the myths we will read about will be about heroes, or legends. Now these heroes were mostly humans, but sometimes they were half-god and half human. Oftentimes the gods would fall in love with humans, and their babies would be half godly and would sometimes even have cool half-godlike powers, like super strength, or super-beauty (which isn't a word yet, but could be in the future don't you think?).

Anyway, the problem with being super strong or super smart was that the other half of you was human, so that half of you would have human type weaknesses. So, you could be very smart, but you could also be so proud that you would offend somebody and then you would be punished for being arrogant.

Other times, you might be strong enough to win all the wars, but you might forget to keep a promise you made to one of the gods, and they would be so mad that they would let something small like a pin-prick kill you.

There was another reason why people loved stories about heroes and legends - it made them feel as though someone other than the moody gods was on their side. They had a person who was one of them, who would be able to fight for the things they believed were important, and fight the gods if necessary, too!

These stories helped people and the society they lived in work the way it was supposed to. It also allowed kings and queens and leaders to pretend they were just like those heroes, so that more people would follow them. Leaders knew that even though they could fight wars and build huge kingdoms, it was the empathy and love these stories taught which kept those kingdoms strong and healthy.

WHERE DO MYTHS COME FROM?

From wherever people are. There are some people who live on deserted islands and still hunt and live all on their own. They don't want to talk to people like us, and scientists believe that if we tried to contact them, they could die of something as harmless as measles (Survival International, 2018)!

Imagine the kind of stories they would have told their children and grandchildren about us: about people who sailed on the sea in large ships, or people who flew in the air on a giant metal bird that had blades for arms! You and I know it is a helicopter, but they wouldn't know that. That's how myths begin and spread, and as they spread; sometimes we discover what we have in common.

Do you remember me telling you about King Arthur at the beginning of this chapter? The legend of King Arthur is a famous one in Great Britain, and the most famous part of it is how he was the only one who was able to pull a magic sword out of the stone to become king (White & Shadbolt, 1998). But did you know that there is a Norse hero named Sigmund who also pulled a magic sword out of a tree, placed there by the god Odin (*Branstock*, n.d.)? We will read more about this particular story later on, but isn't it incredible to realize we have so many stories that echo each other?

Depending on where we live, our stories about what we believe in can be very different, but sometimes the ideas behind the stories are the same. The stories we tell ourselves and our friends can sometimes be so strong, that they can shape how we and others who come after us see the world.

CHAPTER 2: WHO WERE THE NORSE

You see, the word 'Norse' is a mix of languages from old Scandinavia (Scan-dee-nave-ya). Between the years 800 and 1066, Scandinavia was made up of a bunch of countries which today are known as Denmark, Sweden, Iceland, and Norway (Encyclopedia Britannica, 2018). All the people who lived there were called the Norsemen, the Norse, or — and you might have heard this word before – the Vikings.

The Vikings were a fierce but fun-loving lot. Have you heard grown-ups use the phrase, "work hard and party hard"? That's what the Vikings did. They would work from early in the morning to early evening. Some of them would take their ships out to the sea and go fishing, or go looking for new, nicer places to explore and claim, while others would stay behind to grow food, weave cloth, hunt, and sew clothes.

The last part sounds very dull, doesn't it? But did you know the Norse loved colorful clothes and lots of jewelry?

If you showed up in old Scandinavia wearing a pair of blue silk trousers, a red t-shirt, green and blue beads, and orange converse shoes, they would think you were someone very rich and very fashionable (Skov Andersen, 2015)!

Which is why, when the Vikings who had gone out exploring other lands would finally return, they would make it a point to bring all sorts of pretty things for everyone. And then they would gather together in a large space around either a bonfire or an indoor fireplace and they would drink something called mead, eat lots and lots of really nice food, and tell stories.

Some of you might think all of this sitting around and talking was boring, but their stories were anything but boring. They would tell story after story of gods and goddesses who lived in places where it was always either spring or summer, like endless summer holidays, and others who lived in an icy, dark place, like the inside of a freezer.

You see, Scandinavia was, and still is, a place of long, cold winters, and long, dark nights (Stavrou & Tchetchik, 2017). In other parts of the land, during summer, the sun doesn't set at all for months (*Northern Norway – where the sun never sets*, n.d.)!

Imagine how weird that would be - your parents tell you to come home before it gets dark, but since it doesn't grow dark you don't know when to head home! But here's what could have happened.

The Vikings, who were pretty smart, could have waited and watched when the birds began to return to their nests. Or perhaps as they worked, they waited to see when the goats would lie down after what they thought afternoon was. That way they knew it was time to head home and get dinner ready.

They didn't know any other way of life, so it's not surprising that they believed their gods and goddesses lived in lands like theirs, and sometimes with problems like theirs.

So, these were the stories they told each other, and their children and their grandchildren and their great-grand-children and their great-great-grand-children and…well, you get the idea. This was how the myths began and stayed relevant throughout history.

THE NORSE MYTHS

Do you and your friends tell each other stories? Or perhaps your mum tells you stories about what she did when she was your age, and your grandma corrects her. This is how history and myths began. If someone could prove something had happened long ago, then it was written down and it became history. If there was no proof, then people would still write them down but they would call those stories, myths.

And their myths about their gods and goddesses are wonderful! In fact, they even wrote them down in many different ways. Two of the most famous ways are two different kinds of books: a book called the Poetic Edda and the other, called the Prose Edda (Wikipedia Contributors, 2019). The Poetic Edda is one very, very, very long poem about all the gods and the things they did.

Not everyone wanted to read one very long poem, so a man named Snorri Sturluson decided he would try and write them like stories. But, because he lived in the year 1200, the language he used to write the stories was old-fashioned and difficult for anyone over the age of very old.

Some of the stories you're going to read in this book have been taken from the Prose Edda, some from other Norse poems or stories. These were written by people who are not so old, so we can all understand them.

You'll read about dwarfs who live deep underground and make things for the gods, frost giants and their general frostiness, someone who was first a human then a deer, an eight-legged horse (like an octopus horse, but one that can fly!), what the world is really made of (no, it isn't what you think), a god who decides to do something really crazy in exchange for knowledge (ouch!), and so much more.

HOW IT ALL BEGAN

Perhaps you've read about other myths and they explain how the world was created. And if you've read other myths, then you know every story borrows a little from each other and then they tell their version — a little like copycats, but not. But with the norse myths, do me a favour and forget every other story you've heard, because this is unlike any other beginning.

Before anything, and I mean *anything*, including sea and sky and earth and light and noise and even food, there was only fire and ice. That's it. The entire world was made up of fire and ice and nothing nice. In one direction, (no, I don't mean the music band.) was the fire, burning endlessly. If you're going to ask me what was burning, well, I just answered that earlier. Fire. Fire was burning. What was burning in the fire? That is a very good question and one I do not know the answer to. Probably fire. Perhaps you will be the one to find out.

Anyway, the place which was burning was called Muspell. I know your next question. If nothing and nobody existed, then who named this place? The best I can tell you is that they probably named the place *after* everyone came into being. They must've sat down and said, "Well, we can't keep calling it That-Place-of-Endless-Fire, so let's come up with a name." Though between you and me, That-Place-of-Endless-Fire sounds like a super cool name to me, because Muspell isn't pronounced the way it is spelt, oh no. The way the people of Iceland pronounce it is 'Moosh-peth'. Sigh.

On with the story.

In the other direction (which really should've been the name of another band, don't you think?) was ice. What did the ice rest on? MORE ice! It was just ice all the way up, all the way down, and all the way inside and all the way outside. Just ice. And this land of ice was called Niflheim. Which sounds like a sniffle that was startled in the middle, and is pronounced the same way, too. Say it with me: 'Niffle-hime'. Do you see what I mean? And if you think these place names are weird, buckle your godly seatbelts my friends, because we are about to get a *whole* lot weirder.

In between the-place-of-endless-fire or Muspell and Sniffle… sorry, *Niflheim*, lay a huge empty space. A little like the space between your study desk and your bed. You're never sure quite what you want to fill that space with. A beanbag. Maybe a nice rug. A cat-bed. A pillowfort. Clothes that you meant to put away but got knocked off the bed so you've just left them there. The empty space between Muspell and Niflheim was a bit like that. And it was called Ginnungagap. I told you we would get a whole lot weirder with the names, didn't I? I'm sure you're very smart and can say it, but it took me a while to understand that the G-sounds like what it would be if you were saying 'Golly'. Or 'God'. So, it would be pronounced 'Ginh-un-guh-ghap'. It could be a fun game to dare your friends to say it fast about ten times, don't you think? But on with the story. Where were we? Oh yes, Ginnungagap was the empty space between Niflheim and Muspell, except Niflheim also had rivers of ice, but because they were all frozen over, I suppose we could call them river pavements of ice.

Now, if, like me, you are wondering how ice can make rivers before it melts, wonder no more. See, deep, deep, deep below Niflheim was a well. It was so deep, that the word deep had to be invented to describe how deep down it was. This well was called 'Fer-eh-gel-mer' but is written as Hvergelmir. All the rivers came from this well, but by the time they reached Niflheim, they froze into pavements.

It apparently wasn't enough for these pavements to be just made of ice, because they were also full of poison! They were poisoned ice river pavements that wound around Niflheim and reached Ginnungagap. However, on the other side was Muspell, the-place-of-endless-fire, remember? And I'm sure you know what happens when fire and ice meet. The ice melts and if enough ice melts, the fire goes out. That isn't what happened here.

The poison ice river pavement met the heat of Muspell and began to melt. As it melted and the water dripped, the drips magically formed two living beings that were larger than you can imagine, and I'm sure your imagination is incredible. A cow named Audumla (Ay-doo-mlah) and the first ever frost giant who called himself Ymir (Yee-mir). I suppose Ymir named the cow after naming himself because he didn't want to be called Drip. But that might have been a better thing than what came next.

YMIR, HIS SWEATY KIDS, AND A COWLICK

The first thing Ymir did after he came into being, was take a nap. We can all understand that, because naps are nice. But Ymir took a nap near Ginnungagap and because it was so hot he was sweaty (and probably a little stinky, too), which was not so nice. However, Ymir's sweat was magic sweat and his magic sweat turned into his children. I know, EW!

His oldest children were twins, a male giant and a female giant, and they came from the sweat under his left arm. His third child came from the sweat on his legs, and this giant had six heads.

Let's ignore the giant with the six heads, he's not important. Anyway, eventually Ymir's children went on to have many of their own kids, who in turn had more kids, and so on and so forth until there were dozens of frost giants everywhere. They would usually want to hang out with Grandpa Ymir and Audumla the cow, but Audumla did not particularly enjoy this. She'd often wander off on her own in search of much-needed solitude.

One day, after wandering off, Audumla was licking a block of ice and salt. As she kept licking it, she tasted something stringy. So she looked at it and realized there was hair in the ice. She shrugged in a way that only cows can shrug and went on about her day. The next day as she was licking the same salty ice block, she realized that the hair was attached to a man's head. While she was curious, she let it be for that day probably because her mouth was tired and cold. On the third day, she went back and licked at the block until the man's full body emerged.

I'm sure by now you've guessed Audumla's spit was magic spit.

Gross, but effective. It's magic in the same way when there's a bit of dirt on your face and you try to clean it with your palm, it doesn't always go away, but when your mum tries to clean it with a bit of spit on her hanky, your cheek is perfectly clean! Or if you still think it's too gross, think of it as Audumla giving the salty ice block a spit shake.

Audumla's ice-block-spit-shaking son was named Buri (bhoo-rhi) and he was kind, tall, and good-looking. Ymir's kids were anything but. They were probably good-looking, but most of them cruel, unkind, and just plain mean and this made them look ugly.

After Buri had been around for a while, he met a rather nice frost giant and married her and had a son. They named him Bor, but not because they thought he was a bore; they just liked the name. Bor was also lucky enough to marry a nice frost giant named Bestla (Best-lah).

Bestla and Bor had three sons, and they had names you might recognize. Their names were Odin (Oh-din), Vili (Vill-uh), and Ve (Vay). They became the first Aesir (Ice-ir) gods.

THE GODS OF THE AESIR AGE

The Aesir Age. Get it? Because it's pronounced like Ice, and we've all read about the Ice Age in school? It's not funny if I have to explain it.

Moving on. The Aesir age started when Odin, Vili, and Ve decided to go exploring. Except they didn't have anywhere to go except into the nothingness of Ginnungagap. After they had explored some of the nothing, they went further and found more nothing. This was a problem. Which is also why when you ask someone if something is wrong, and they answer "nothing", they're probably right. Ginnungagap was a big space of nothing, and nothing was a problem.

Odin, Vili, and Ve wanted to do something about it, so they went to ask Ymir if they could use their new godly powers to make stuff. Ymir said no. When they asked why, he told them because he liked saying no. Then he went back to lazing around and doing absolutely zero things. The three brothers thought this was unfair. If Ymir wasn't going to do anything, the least he could do was let them do something. They tried to tell him this, but Ymir shouted at them and told them to go away before he hit them. This wasn't anything new, because Ymir and most of his frost giant kids were horrible, violent, and wicked. They picked fights and were mean to people just because they thought it was fun. Do you know people like them? They are the sort of people who are unkind to others because they think it is fun, or because they think it makes them look stronger. You and I know better. It doesn't.

Odin, Vili, and Ve also knew better, but their solution was a little extreme. They decided to attack him, and after a long fight during which no one was sure who would win, Odin managed to stab him. But because he was larger than anything in the universe, he had a lot of blood in him. In fact, he had so much blood, that when Odin stabbed him, all of it began to flow out and become a flood that drowned all of the frost giants that were wicked like him.

But one of them named Bergelmir (Bear-gil-mer) and his wife hid from the flood in a hollow tree trunk. Then they had the bright idea to turn it into a boat and sail away. "Sail away where?", you ask? To Jotunheim (Yo-tun-hime), of course. "But where's Jotunheim?", you ask me again. It's going to be formed in a bit. "How can they sail away to a place that doesn't exist yet!?", you ask. My, you certainly have a lot of questions, don't you? Well, as they're sailing away, Odin, Vili, and Ve get busy working on everything. And before you ask me any other questions, just wait for a minute. Some of them will be answered in the next chapter.

After Bergelmir and his wife sailed away, they promised they would never forgive any of the gods for killing Ymir. When they had children and grandchildren and great-grandchildren, all of them also never forgave or forgot, and they became enemies with the gods forever.

THE WORLD IS LIKE A BODY

Now, you would think Odin, Vili, and Ve would at least hold a funeral for Ymir, but no. They knew Ymir's body was full of magic, so they shoved his body into Ginnungagap. And then they set to work. They created the world from what's left of him. Yes, you heard me correctly. While the lesson here is 'don't kill people and definitely don't do what Odin and his brothers did', at least they used every part of Ymir instead of wasting anything!

His flesh became the earth and his bones turned into mountains. This is probably why they're so bumpy. His teeth turned into rocks, which isn't really as surprising as it should be since some rocks are made of calcium — the same stuff teeth are made of. But perhaps a god's teeth were made of something else? Rocks, probably.

Anyway, what's left? Plenty, actually. Hold on to your seats for a minute. If you're not sitting down, hold on to the wall for a minute because do you know what part of him was made into the rivers? His blood. I suppose we should all be grateful that Ymir had very odd colored blood.

They made his hair into trees, and this is the really crazy part. They played volley-ball with his skull for a bit before kicking it up so high that it got stuck there and became the sky! But I guess they forgot to take his brains out of the skull, because the next thing you know, his brains floated out of his skull, and instead of following the rules of gravity and falling to the ground, instead they turned into clouds!

So the next time someone tells you that the clouds are made of water vapor and air, you can tell them the truth. Clouds are made up of *brains*. Which also explains all the squiggly lines of the clouds! Have you ever seen a cloud that is a straight line? No. That just proves it.

I have to admire the three brothers for not wasting even a little bit of what they thought would be useful in creating the world. This could be why the Norse are so eco-friendly about the things they use.

THE SUN, THE MOON, THE STARS, AND THE END

After the three brothers had finished creating the world, they decided the skull - I'm sorry, I meant the *sky* - up there looked empty. To sort this out, they wandered over to the edge of Muspell and sat staring at the fire.

As the fire burnt endlessly, it suddenly shot sparks into the air, and all three brothers had the same idea at the same time. They decided to catch some of the sparks and throw it into the sky to make stars, and they did just that.

They looked at the skull-sky and thought it needed something more. They decided to go into Muspell and see what else they could find to use over there, instead of using whatever was left of Ymir.

So, they went into Muspell and were wandering around, when suddenly they heard a great booming voice. "WHO ARE YOU AND WHAT DO YOU WANT?" the voice said. The brothers were confused, because they thought they were the only ones around and Muspell was supposed to be empty, so instead of answering the question, they yelled back "TELL US WHO YOU ARE FIRST, THEN WE'LL THINK ABOUT ANSWERING YOU!" Now, first of all, this is a rude way to answer a question, especially when you are exploring a place you are not supposed to be in. But because they are gods, I suppose the rules don't apply to them, or they hadn't been invented yet.

The voice was a little annoyed when it replied, "YOU CAME TO *MY* HOUSE, SO YOU TELL ME FIRST!" Now, even though they had been rude at first, Odin and his brothers had been brought up by

Bor and Bestla to be polite. They realized they weren't behaving very well, so they remembered what their parents had taught them and answered politely, "We are sorry Mr. Voice. Our names are Odin, Ville, and Ve and we are the Aseir. We've just finished creating the world and were looking for something else we could create."

"Hmm. Like what?" asked Mr. Voice.

"Well, we aren't quite sure. You wouldn't happen to have something shiny, would you?" answered the brothers.

"I might," said Mr. Voice. "Let me show you around."

The brothers heard loud footsteps coming towards them. The footsteps were so loud, the ground shook with every thump.

Soon, Mr. Voice stood before them and they looked up. And they looked up. And they looked up some more. Finally, when they had looked so far up, there was not much 'up' left to look at, and they saw his face. His face was made of *fire*.

They gulped, and took a deep breath. Then because they were gods and gods were not supposed to show fear, and also because their parents had taught them to be polite, they just smiled and said hello.

Mr. Voice looked at them and said, "I suppose I should introduce myself. My name is Surt."

Odin almost asked him where the rest of his name was, but thankfully Ville stomped on his foot, and Ve shook his head at him. Ville spoke, "It's nice to meet you, Mr. Surt. Would you show us what you think we could use? Please," he added quickly, because some words are magic words even if they aren't god magic.

"Of course!" Surt replied and led them to a pool of what looked like hot, melted gold. Ve dipped his hands in it. It *was* hot, melted gold!

The brothers were ecstatic, which is a word for very very happy. They thanked Surt over and over again and began to pack some of the gold away.

Surt was curious. "What are you going to make with that?" he asked them.

"We thought we would try and create a sun chariot and a moon chariot," they replied.

"Oh," said Surt. He thought for a moment. "That's all very well, but who will draw the chariot? I don't think you can make the chariot self-driving, after all, Artificial Intelligence hasn't been created yet."

"We've thought of that," said Ville. "We're going to create horses and then we're going to invite someone we know to drive it across the sky in an endless race."

"Interesting," said Surt. "But, there's just one problem." "You do realize the fire and gold of Muspell is so hot, that the chariot will end up burning whatever is on the ground, right?"

The brothers looked at each other. They looked at Surt. Surt looked back at them. Then they looked at each other some more.

In the middle of all of this looking, Ve had an idea. "What if we cool the moon chariot down enough, so that the fire is almost out and the gold is so light it looks like silver?" Ville and Odin liked that idea. In fact they liked it so much that Odin had an idea of his own. "What if," he exclaimed, "we put a shield under the sun chariot, so that the sun only warms the world instead of burning it up?" (*NORSE GODS: SÓL – Ýdalir*, n.d.)

Everyone was delighted with both these ideas. Everyone, that is, except Surt. "Hey, you three, we've still got a problem," he said somewhat unhappily. "Now that you're going to create things, you do know I'm going to have to destroy all that you've created right along with all of you, don't you?"

"Right now?" the brothers asked.

"Oh no! Not for thousands and thousands of years!" Surt reassured them. The brothers looked at each other and shrugged.

"That's alright then," they said. "Ragnarok (Rahg-nuh-rok) has to happen sometime. Everything has to begin for everything to end and for everything to begin again." (*Ragnarok | Encyclopedia.com*, 2019)

"Oh phew! No hard feelings then?" Surt asked, relieved.

"No, no, none at all," they replied.

They all said a cheery goodbye to Surt and went back to Ymir-Land to start making the sun and moon chariots. After they'd finished making them, they went to find Sol (Soul) and Mani (Maah-ni).

Sol and Mani were Mundilfari's (Min-thil-fa-rey) children. Mundilfari was the god of time. Where were Mundilfari and his kids while Ymir was being born? At a guess, I would say they were existing outside of time. How can you exist outside of time, you ask? Well, have you ever sat watching the clock on your classroom wall, on the last day of school just before summer vacation begins?

The clock ticks and the clock tocks and it feels as though you're living in the space between the tick and the tock.

That's probably where Mundilfari and his kids were living, too. In the space between Ginnungagap and Ymir, which was the creation version of the tick and the tock.

Odin, Ville, and Ve went up to Sol and Mani and asked them if they'd like a job. By this time Sol and Mani were sick of just sitting around all day with nothing to do, so the minute they were asked, they said yes. The brothers told them they would need to make a full circle around the world every twenty-four hours. Without hesitation, Sol climbed into the sun chariot, Mani climbed into the moon-chariot, and away they went. And that is how the hours were divided into night and day.

Another interesting little tidbit is this. Did you know certain days of the week are named after Sol and Mani? Because Sol is also called Sunna in Old German, the best day of the week, Sunday, is named after her, while the first day of the week, Monday, is named after Mani.

CHAPTER 3: THE NINE WORLDS

According to some people, Bor and Bestla planted a tree long before the brothers were born. Now, as you've probably guessed, this was no ordinary tree. This was Yggdrasil (Ig-drah-sil), the hugest, largest, most giganta-enorma-saurus magic tree that ever existed or will exist. It was so huge, that instead of Ginnungagap, Yggdrasil became the center of the universe.

THE WORLD TREE IS ALSO NAMED YGGRASIL

After it became the center of the universe, it continued to grow so much that both Niflheim and Muspell became part of the tree!

But did it stop there? No. Oh no, it didn't. It grew and grew and grew, the same way your younger sibling who was once shorter than you, grows taller than you. But Yggdrasil was super-magic, because you know how most trees grow fruit, or have nests in their branches? Yggdrasil instead had whole, entire worlds resting on them! Nine worlds, to be exact. This is also why sometimes it is called The World Tree.

All of these nine worlds were connected to each other because of Yggdrasil. Which are these worlds? Well, you already know both Nifleheim and Muspell; the others are Asgard (Ahs-guard), Midgard (Mid-guard), Jotunheim (Yo-tun-hime), Vanaheim (Vah-na-hime), Alfheim (Alf-hime), Svartalfheim (Svuck-tarv-hime), and Helheim (Hale-hime).

You might be wondering how a tree is strong enough to hold all of that plus all those humans, animals, grass, and trees — do you think the trees in those worlds would be baby Yggdrasil trees? Sorry, I got distracted. I think the answer could be that because Yggdrasil grew so big, it became the universe. And as you know and have probably learnt in your science classes, the universe can hold many, many different kinds of worlds, all at the same time. Perhaps when you grow up, you will discover a different answer.

Some of you might be wondering whether Ymir's skull, which made up the sky, was on the outside of the tree or on the inside. Again, I think it was both.

"That's impossible!" you cry. I know it sounds like that, but hear me out. Think of it like bubble-wrap. You know, the kind that you unwrap from something and start popping the bubbles? That. Imagine you've got a piece of bubble-wrap and a mug. Now you know that the bubble-wrap is smooth on the outside, but has bubbles on the inside. When you wrap the outside of your mug, the mug can feel the bubbles. But when you fold the wrap over *inside* the mug, it feels the smooth side of the bubble wrap. That is how I think it works. Do you have any ideas on how it might work?

Anyway, let us get back to Yggdrasil. Between the branches of the tree were many animals. You know how some of the trees you have seen on walks or while camping will have birds, squirrels, and snakes? The World Tree is not so different in that way. There are many animals who live in it, but the four main ones you should know about are the no-name giant Eagle and his friend Vedrfolnir (Vey-thruh-vol-ner) the hawk, Ratatoskr (Rat-tuh-tos-ker) the mean squirrel, and Nidhogg (New-thong) the evil snake-dragon.

Among the others who live in the tree are four deer which represent the four winds, and a goat and a stag. They dash around on the tree's branches like they're in a race and eat all its leaves. The goat, whose name is Heidrun (Hi-dhoon), provides the warriors of Valhalla with an endless supply of something called mead. The stag is named Eikthyrnir (Eykh-thir-nir), and he spends his entire day eating the new, young leaves of The World Tree.

But let's talk about the first four — the eagle, the hawk, the squirrel, and the snake-dragon. These four are not friends, except for no-name Eagle and Vedrfolnir who lives on top of no-name Eagle's head. That might sound uncomfortable, but because the Eagle is pretty gigantic and Vedrfolnir is *mostly* normal sized, Vedrfolnir has plenty of space to relax in.

He also flies all around and brings back news about what's happening where. You know that one time you stuck your finger in your nose when you thought no-one was looking? Vedrfolnir probably saw you and told the eagle. But don't worry, I'm sure eagles do the same in their own eagle way, too.

Next is Ratatoskr, the mean, gossipy little trouble maker. Why am I saying nasty things about him? Because he truly is a tattle-tale. The trouble he creates is his main job. Everytime he hears no-name Eagle insult Nidhogg, he runs down The World Tree to where Nidhogg lives and tells him all that Eagle said. Perhaps the eagle may have said something like, "I think Nidhogg has a fat head."

Ratatoskr would immediately run down the tree, march over to where Nidhogg would be nibbling at the roots of the tree because he wanted to destroy it, and be all, "Bro, did you hear? Eagle called you a great big stinking fathead who likes to laze around doing nothing!"

At which point, Nidhogg growls, snarls, and sputters, "Well... well, you can tell that birdbrain, he looks like a *feather duster!*" So, off Ratatoskr would go. He would climb up the tree till he reached the top and tell Eagle what Nidhogg had said, but he would add to it and lie about what was actually said, making them even more mad at each other. And then all three of them would do it over and over again.

The thing is, Eagle is supposed to be very wise, but I don't think it's smart to pick a fight with someone. Especially based on the lies of someone else. Moral of the story: Don't trust Ratatoskr. He is a lying liar who lies.

FIVE PLUS FOUR WORLDS SITTING IN A TREE

That makes exactly n-i-n-e!

Okay, I may be bad at poetry, but I do know some things about the nine worlds that are a part of The World Tree. Let's take a look at all of them one-by-one, starting with the ones who get a nice view of everything at the top, and the ones who get a different sort of view at the bottom:

ASGARD: THE PLACE THE AESIR CALL HOME

Asgard is the home of all the Aesir gods and goddesses. Which is why, it is no surprise it's got the best view of everything, all high up in the sky among all the brain clouds. Every god and goddess has their own mansion made of gold and silver, and Odin is the ruler of Asgard and the supreme leader of the Aesir.

Odin's mansion has a huge inner mansion, or hall, called Valhalla (Vahl-ha-lah). This is where half the good people who died in battle go. The other half go to another nice place called Fólkvangr (Fork-vahn-gur) which is ruled by the goddess Freya. You must be wondering why only the people who died in battle go to these nice places. You see, battles can be any kind of battle. They could be someone saving another person from getting crushed by a car, it could be someone who is sad, lonely, and upset deciding not to give up and keep on living ~~kill themselves~~, or it could be someone standing up and being a decent person when no one else is.

A battle is simply a fight you have inside yourself when some part of you wants to do something mean, and will hurt both you and someone else, while the other part of you wants to do the decent thing and be firm but kind. If you die in the middle of doing something good and honest for someone else, the gods of Valhalla or Folkvangr will welcome you with open arms.

Every night, Valhalla has a party to celebrate all the new people who arrive and they swap stories with the others who have been there. The new people are brought to Valhalla by the Valkyries (Val-kuh-rees). Valkyries ride flying horses and decide who gets to go to Valhalla and who doesn't. Everyone loves hanging out in

Valhalla because it is pretty incredible. The roof is made up of gold shields, while the pillars on which they rest are actual spears!

Folkvangr is Freya's place for warriors. Unlike Valhalla, Folkvangr is a large meadow where the sun shines, but the weather is always the perfect temperature and instead of the type of party in Valhalla, the people who go there tend to have very fun picnics.

As you can see, Asgard is a wonderful place. One out of three of Yggdrasil's massive roots reaches into The Well of Urd (Oord), also known as the river of fate, which lies deep underground in Asgard and is guarded and watered by three ladies known as The Norn (rhymes with *corn*).

Odin and his wife Queen Frigg (Free-guh), rule it and fill it with wonderful things made either by them, or by others - such as the wall around Asgard. What's so wonderful about a wall? The fact that it was built through trickery! Which is not a *good* thing, but when you're a god, people tend to say most of the things you've done are amazing. We'll read about that in a couple of chapters.

VANAHEIM: HOME OF THE VANIR

For the Vanir, the land of Vanaheim was home. Who were the Vanir? They were an ancient group of gods – gods as old as the Aesir. They were the ones who cared most about things like health, growing things, and wealth. They were and are masters of witchcraft and magic, and every single person knew that the Vanir had the ability to correctly tell the future. Though they could and did fight, they were not known as gods and goddesses of battle like the Aesir. They preferred to do a little gardening, or maybe learn new ways of improving things, and they liked making, buying, or selling pretty and expensive stuff. The most famous of all the Vanir were Njord (Nigh-ord) and his two children, Freyr (Fray), and Freyja (Fray-yah), who came to Asgard as a sign of peace.

The story goes that a Vanir named Gullveig (Gool-Vag-uh) was among some of the best witches who practiced a form of magic called seidr (say-dur). Seidr is magic which allows you to see and sometimes shape the future. Gullveig wandered from place to place showing people her seidr skills, and occasionally teaching them, too.

When she reached Asgard, they invited her to stay and show off her seidr skills. Except, the more she used them, the more the Aesir gods began to want only that. They wanted it so much, in fact, that they grew selfish and began to forget the things which made them loved and respected by the people in the first place - things such as loyalty, honor, and doing the right thing. They no longer valued what they were good at or the qualities that made them who they were, and were instead focused on what they didn't have.

Except, instead of accepting the fact that it was their fault, instead they decided to blame Gullveig for their actions. In fact, they blamed her so much, they decided the only way for them to stop behaving so badly was for them to kill her. No Gullveig, they thought, no more problem.

So, they gathered a lot of wood and they burnt her. But, she stepped out of the fire as though she was stepping out onto a beach. They got some more wood, and burnt her again, but she yawned and stepped out of the dying fire as though she was bored when actually she was very angry. But she would give them one more chance to stop behaving in this manner.

However, the Aesir were furious — which is another word for super angry – that their plan had not worked. So, this time, they got more and more and more wood to make sure the fire would be hot and would burn properly. And this time when they shoved Gullveig into it, she burnt down to ash.

The Aesir were very happy and were sure that now their problems were over. Except, they weren't. They were only beginning.

They heard a whooshing noise behind them, and when they turned to look, the ashes swirled up into a pillar, and the pillar of ash transformed into Gullveig. By now, she was so angry, she could barely talk.

Have you ever been that angry? So angry that all the words you want to say seem to burn up in your blood before they even reach your mouth? Gullveig was that angry.

Instead of saying anything, she turned around and stormed away all the way back to Vanaheim and told everyone there exactly what had happened. Njord, who was the leader of the Vanir, was even more angry than Gullveig and told everyone in Vanaheim to get ready for war against the Aesir.

The Aesir knew they had messed up, but instead of accepting

what they did was wrong and saying they were sorry, they thought the best way to deal with this was to go to war against the Vanir.

So, they fought against each other. The Aeisr used battle strategies to fight, while the Vanir used some battle strategy and some magic. People on both sides died, but eventually it looked as though the Vanir might win.

At this point, Odin sat down with the other Aesir and said, "Look guys, I know we thought we were doing the right thing, but clearly not. We were wrong and we should tell them so, or this war will go on forever." Some of the other Aesir weren't sure if they wanted to stop, but Odin simply said, "Well, too bad. I'm the King and what I say goes, so you can deal with it."

Of course, if he'd just said this right at the beginning, there might not have been so many problems, but then we would also not have had a story.

Anyway, both the Vanir and the Aesir called a truce. And as a sign they wouldn't fight with each other anymore, they sent people from their land to live with the others. The Aesir sent Hoenir (High-neer) and Mimir (Mee-meer), two of Odin's relatives and friends, to live with the Vanir. The Vanir sent Njord, Frey, and Freya to live with the Aesir.

After this, while there were small fights, there was no war between both these places – even when the Vanir cut off Mimir's head. But that's a story for another day. Since no one really knows the exact location of the land of Vanaheim, or even what it looks like, that is also probably why no one went to challenge them to a war again!

ALFHEIM: WHERE THE PRETTY ELVES LIVE

Alfheim (Alf-hime) means home of the Elves. It is roughly close to where Asgard is on The World Tree. Alfheim is where all the elves live and these elves are the most beautiful creatures you've ever seen. This is why they are called light elves, because they are so beautiful to look at, and it feels as though you are looking directly at a light bulb. You know how if you look directly at a light-bulb, you can't look at it too long, so you close your eyes, but it feels as though you can still feel the light and see the shape of the bulb in your mind? That's what it felt like to look at the elves of Alfheim.

The leader of the elves was the Vanir god Frey and he ruled the land of Alfheim. Frey was as powerful as Odin and Thor, and was also the god of summer and fertility, which is a word for growing things. Even though Frey could fight as fiercely as Thor, he didn't like to fight unless he had no other choice. He was a kind and happy god who preferred to look after nature and help others learn how to do the same. The elves were also gods, but they weren't as powerful as any of the others like the Aesir and the Vanir. They used what little power they had to take care of nature and made sure all growing things were fruitful.

They weren't always nice to humans, but would also try to help them because Frey didn't want them to be mean. They knew how to make humans fall sick, and they knew how to heal them. The elves and Frey also loved poetry and the arts and music, so they would wait to see which human seemed to have talent. Then, they would help that human think of words for their poem or story, or see the colors they needed for their art in their mind's eye. So, if you ever wanted to act, dance, or paint something, you would ask Frey for help. Then, he would make sure the elves of Alfheim who were good at the stuff you wanted help with, would give you the inspiration you needed to make your art.

Today, a large number of people think Alfheim was just another word for fairyland, while some people think that is where all of our stories about fairies and elves come from (*Álfheimr*, 2021). What do you think? Do you think Alfheim and Fairyland are the same place? Perhaps, you will be the one to find out!

NIFLHEIM: ICE HERE, ICE THERE, ICE ICE EVERYWHERE

We've already read about Niflheim, so I'm sure you remember what it is all about. Think of it like the old rhyme "Old Mac'Donald":

On Yggdrasil's branch was a land, Niflheim was its name!

With an ice block here, and a river there,

Here an ice, there an ice, everywhere an ice, ice.

On Yggdrasil's branch was a land, Niflheim was its name!

You also know about the snake-dragon called Nidhug who lives there and nibbles away at one of Yggdrasil's roots. Though why he wants to eat an uncooked root is between him and his taste-buds. The same way some people like eating kiwi on pizza...yuck.

Moving on.

We also read about the river or well named Hvergelmir. This river is the river from which all living things come and the place where all living things will go back. One of Yggdrasil's three roots is also watered by this spring, which probably explains why it is always so green.

CHAPTER 4: MORE ABOUT THE WORLDS OF THE WORLD TREE

W e've already read about some of the worlds, especially about the ice world. Now let's read about the other worlds, starting with the one that is the opposite of ice.

MUSPEL: IT'S ON FIRE

Do you remember reading about Muspel? The place where Odin, Ville, and Ve went for a little trip, ended up meeting the fire giant Surt and let's see, what else? Oh yes, the land was on FIRE!

By now, Muspel had minor fire demons and other fire giants. I mean, Surt probably got bored waiting to destroy the world at Ragnarok and created some of the demons out of lava or something, and maybe he found a nice fire giant to marry and they had fire giant children. I don't know for sure, but I'm guessing that's what happened.

Just to recap, which means to repeat the main points of an explanation (*recap*, n.d.), Muspel is a fiery hot place and everywhere you look, there are lava rivers, mile-high flames which shoot sparks, and it looks mysterious because of all the smoke and also because all the walls are covered with soot. It is ruled by Surtr, who is waiting for Ragnarok to arrive, so he can go out and destroy Asgard and everything else.

I have to say, though, I'm sure the heat of Muspel makes for a great barbecue place — as long as we aren't the ones getting barbecued.

MIDGARD: THE HUMAN HOME

Midgard is also called Middle Earth because it sits right in the middle of The World Tree. It is below Asgard, and because the gods like to visit us often, Midgard and Asgard are connected by a bridge. But like everything else with the gods, the bridge is no ordinary bridge. It is called the Bifrost (Bif-roast). It is also called the Rainbow Bridge, because it is made of, you guessed it, a rainbow!

The bridge starts in Asgard, goes over the ocean which surrounds Midgard and ends up in locations wherever the gods decide. The ocean surrounding Midgard has a serpent living in it. The serpent is so big, it can curl its body all the way around the world without having to stretch! Not something you should think about the next time you're at the beach and some seaweed clings to your legs. If you think that is scary for you, think of how scary it must have been for Ask and Embla, who were the first humans. "But can the giant serpent get out? And where did Ask and Embla come from?" You cry. To answer the first part of that question, no. The giant serpent won't leave the ocean until the end of the world arrives. If you're at the beach and you see a snake head as large as a jumbo jet come out of the water, you'll know it's the end of the world. As for the second question? Patience, my gentle reader. We are soon coming to those stories. Read on, read on.

JOTUNHEIM: A GIGANTIC HOME

Jotunheim is the home of the giants. Not just any giants, but the frost giants. You remember - the ones who are the grandchildren of Ymir. They're the ones who promised themselves that they would remain the enemies of the Aesir gods forever and ever until Ragnarok, when they will all be busy fighting each other.

Not all frost giants hated the gods. Some of them were even invited to live in Asgard and were also called gods, like Loki (Low-key), the god of mischief. Some of the giants married gods and had children with them. Frey married Gerd (Gear-d), Njord married Skadi (Skah-di), and so on. The gods didn't much like visiting Jotunheim, but then they were used to beautiful lands where the grass was always green, and the sun was shining, and everything looked like a photograph. Jotunheim was not like that. What is Jotunheim like, then?

Well, Jotunheim is made up of mostly rocks, ice, snow, and thick forests where the trees grow so close to each other, you have to hold your breath, suck your stomach in, squeeze through them sideways, and hope you don't get stuck. It also has the ocean on one side and is separated from Asgard by the river Ifingr (Ee-ving-er) on the other. This river doesn't ever freeze over, flows very fast, and is deep enough to drown a giant, so the giants can't cross over to Asgard. The third water source is the spring of wisdom, better known as Mimir's Well, and it sits deep under Jotunheim watering the third root of The World Tree.

Since the ground in Jotunheim is rocky, pebbly, and hard, thanks to the cold, no one can plant anything or have any kind of a farm, despite the water from the river. So, the giants go fishing and hunting twice or three times in a single day, because they're giants and they have to eat as much as I imagine giants need to eat. Which is probably a hundred times more than you and me.

SVARTALFHEIM: THE HOME UNDER THE GROUND

Svartalfheim (Svuck-tarv-hime), is the underground home of the dwarves. Dwarves cannot live above ground because if they come in contact with sunlight, they turn to stone. For this reason, they live inside hollowed-out rocks, deep inside caves, or create underground tunnels which connect to underground homes.

The dwarves can create things no one else can — not even the gods! They are such skilled crafters that they can make any sort of weapon or treasure, and have, in fact, made many of the weapons and jewelry which the gods of Asgard have in their keeping. They created jewelry such as the magical ring Draupnir (Drope-near), and hair for the goddess Sif (rhymes with *tiff*) — yes, *hair*. They also made weapons such as Odin's spear Gungnir (Goong-near) and Thor's famous hammer Mjolnir (Myol-near).

But, where did the dwarves come from? Well, that's a story I can't wait to tell you. And I won't. Wait, I mean; sorry. Here goes.

Do you remember when Odin, Ville, and Ve shoved Ymir's body into Ginnungagap? And after they'd finished building the world from parts of him, they left his remains to rot. As his flesh was rotting, worms started to crawl out of it and guess who those worms turned into? That's right. *Dwarves*!

Anyway, once the gods saw this happening, they decided to help the worms — sorry — *dwarves* along, and gave them intelligence and skills and shapeshifting abilities and other useful stuff. Then, they asked for volunteers for a special task which could possibly turn those volunteers to stone. The task was to hold up Ymir's skull which formed the sky. So, four dwarves named Nordri (Norduh-ri), Sudri (Shud-rih), Austri (Esh-tri), and Vestri (Wes-tri) went off to hold up the sky. And *that* my friends, is where we get the directions North, South, East, and West from.

The other dwarves probably didn't want to be picked for any other such tasks, so they thanked the gods politely, and went off underground where the gods wouldn't be able to find them in a hurry.

HELHEIM: WHERE THE DEAD GO ON LIVING

The name sounds scary, doesn't it? Don't worry. Helheim is not a bad place, nor is it *not* a place where all the dead people go to be punished. The bad dead people are punished and cursed by the gods in different ways, but all those who died of old age, illness, or anything other than battle or drowning, go to Helheim.

Helheim is ruled by the goddess Hel, and while she is scary to look at, she is also very wise, just, and kind. In this place, once the dead people arrive, they simply go on and live the lives they did while they were alive (*Hel (The Underworld) - Norse Mythology for Smart People*, 2012). In Helheim, you can continue to do things like swimming, meeting your friends — if they're also there — for a meal, working, or taking a nice long nap. It wasn't a constantly happy, exciting place like Folksvangr or Valhalla, but it wasn't a sad, unhappy place either. It was just more like life after death in a place you didn't expect.

OTHER FACTS ABOUT THE WORLD TREE

As you can see, those are the nine realms, and how they are connected and placed in The World Tree!

The Norns

In addition to this, while you know Yggdrasil is cared for by the Norns, did you also know that if they don't water it from the Well of Urd, the universe will begin to fade away? However, watering the tree is only one half of their job.

The other half of their job is to weave a tapestry. A tapestry is a cloth which has a scene or a picture woven into it with lots and lots of different threads. Each thread the Norns use are said to belong to a living being — including the gods. When the Norns have finished using your thread in the tapestry, they cut the thread and that is when you die.

The Numbers Game

The numbers three and nine, are an important part of Norse culture and mythology (Skjalden, 2020).

The number three is a holy number for the Norse, because of the three brothers who created the world. It is also important because the three Norns take care of every person's fate, and also because when the war with the Vanir ended, three of the most important and powerful Vanir became part of Asgard.

Add those together and you get the number nine. Nine was said to be the number of Magic. You know there are nine lands, but there are also other things that make that particular number important. When Odin wanted to learn something called rune magic, he hung from The World Tree for nine whole days! When Heimdall was born, he had nine mothers. Yes, nine mothers! And afterwards everyone knew his birth was a very special event because of all that he would do in his human life and his godly life.

CHAPTER 5: HUMANS, GODS, AND MONSTERS

Well, so far we've read about the creation of the world and we've read the names of gods we don't know yet. Don't worry — that's what we're going to read about now.

CREATION OF HUMANS

After Odin, Vile, and Ve had finished creating most of the world, they were taking a walk through Midgard, and were admiring all they'd done. Gods are like this. They like to admire what they've made, just like us. Unlike us, if people don't say nice things about what they've made, they tend to lose their temper and fight or curse everyone. But since there wasn't anyone around to say nice or nasty things, they complimented each other and were happy.

They admired the sparkling rivers, the mighty mountains, the green, green fields, and the blue skull-sky. They stopped, took a look around, patted each other on the back, and then twisted around and patted themselves on the back. Pat, pat, pat. "Good job, brother!" said one happily.

"Don't you mean, 'God job?'" snickered the other.

"Goodly godly job!" chuckled the third.

It was a good thing no one was around to tell them their jokes were terrible.

Vile took a look around again. He began to smile, but frowned instead. "What's wrong, Vile?" asked Odin. "I'm not sure, but something doesn't feel right." Answered Vile. "Hmm. You're right" said Ve. "Feels like something is missing, but what could it be?"

Odin looked around too. Then Vile looked around in another direction. Ve looked around in a third direction. Then they all switched places and looked again.

"I've got it!" said Odin excitedly.

"Tell us, quick!" said the other two in unison.

"Walls," said Odin. He was proud of himself for figuring it out.

"Walls?" asked Ve. He wasn't sure Odin had found the solution.

"Walls?" asked Vile. He wasn't sure what was going on.

"Walls," Odin nodded determinedly. "See, we've made a beautiful world here. But do you know who's going to want to live here?"

Vile understood immediately. "Giants," he said in an understanding tone.

"Giants?" asked Ve in confusion. He still didn't get it.

"Frost giants, to be precise," replied Odin. "They will want to find a way to move here instead of staying in Jotunheim. Except, if they move here, they will ruin *everything*."

"Oh. Oh no!" Ve was horrified. "They'll break all the trees!"

"They'll muddy up the rivers!" cried Vile. "They'll tear up the grass and make the ground all icy and horrid!"

"Yes," Odin said grimly. "That is why we need walls!"

"You're right!" said Ve.

"That's all very well, but what could be strong enough to keep out the giants?" asked Vile.

"Eyebrows!" exclaimed Ve.

"*Eyebrows?*" Odin said in disbelief, raising his own..

"Can all of us please stop repeating everything the other says?" huffed Ve in irritation. "We sound like a video stuck on pause."

"What's a video?" asked Odin.

"What's a pause?" asked Vile.

"It hasn't been invented yet, and that's not what is important," said Ve, shaking his head.

"Okay. Let's go back to the eyebrow wall idea," Odin suggested.

"Look, if we turned Ymir's skull into the sky and it was big enough to cover the whole world, then it stands to reason his eyebrows will be useful," reasoned Ve.

"Good point, Ve! Let's go get this done," Vile said. Then he turned to Odin and whispered, "so what *is* a pause?"

"It's like a stop, but only for a minute." Odin whispered back. "Wouldn't that just be a stop?" asked Vile in confusion. "No, when you stop, you have to start from the beginning. When you pause, you can pick up from where you left off," said Odin. "Now hurry, or Ve will yell at us again." And he hurried away.

The brothers went to Ginunngagap, plucked out Ymir's eyebrows, planted them like trees all around Midgard, and they turned into a wall no one could break through, including the frost giants.

The brothers were very pleased with themselves and they went to Asgard to check on how they wanted their palaces and halls built, and also to take a break. After a while, they went to look at Midgard again, decided they had done a good job again, and patted themselves on their backs *again.*

It still didn't feel quite right to Vile, but he didn't say anything. He was trying to pause his thoughts and start them again.

It didn't feel right to Ve, but he didn't say anything. He was wondering if the walls would grow bushy like regular eyebrows do.

It didn't feel right to Odin, but he didn't say anything. He still wanted to know what a video was.

As they were walking along the beach, all three of them tripped on a tree trunk.

"Why would anyone put that there?" Odin said crossly.

"Who would put that there?" said Ve grumpily. "It's not as though there's anyone around except us."

"That's it!" Vile was excited. "That's what Midgard is missing, you guys! Let's make *people*."

The other two were thrilled. "Vile, you're a genius!"

They decided to make the first ever humans out of the driftwood they had tripped over. This could also be why when people use the phrase, "knock on wood" to avoid bad luck, they knock on their own skulls, because according to the Norse, we are like Pinocchio.

So, the brothers made the first humans. Odin gave them the breath of life, while Vile and Ve made their brains work. Then the brothers blessed the humans with creativity, speech, sight, movement and so on, before hurriedly making them some very pretty clothes.

The man was named Ask (Aye-sk), and the woman was named Embla (Ehm-bla). Then the brothers gave Ask and Embla the whole of Midgard, so they could make it their home. That's how they became the parents of the entire human race.

Science will tell you we evolved from monkeys, and that could be as true as anything else. It depends on what you want to believe. If you like monkeys, you can decide that's where you came from.

If you like trees, you can decide that's where you came from. And the next time you look at a tree, you can thank the three brothers that they decided to make humans, instead of furniture.

WHERE BAD POETS COME FROM

Odin and his brothers left Midgard to the care of Ask and Embla and went back to Asgard. As they were walking across the Bifrost, the sparkly rainbow bridge, Vile and Ve were talking about the things they were thinking of doing back at Asgard. They also wanted to spend time with their children and with the gods and goddesses who were beginning to make Asgard their home.

Odin, however, was planning an adventure. He loved to know things. The more things he knew, the more he could become better at them. The better he was at whatever he knew, the happier he was. And a happy Odin, was a not-so-dangerous Odin, which was a good thing.

On this adventure, he had decided to try and get The Mead of Poetry from the giants. What is The Mead of Poetry? The Mead of Poetry is a drink made from the blood of Kvasir (Kwey-see-urh), who was murdered by two horrid dwarves for being the wisest and most intelligent of all the gods. After they murdered him, they mixed his blood with honey and kept it in three barrels to sell as an energy drink for your brain. Or super-smart-brain-juice. And if you think that's gross, just you wait my friends, because we are about to get more gross than you could ever imagine.

After the dwarves had murdered him and made Kvasir honey juice, they hid it away because they didn't want the Aesir gods to know what had happened. But the two dwarves were the kind of people who would quarrel with others and then murder them. This is what they ended up doing when a giant and his wife came visiting. First, they sat down to supper. Then they picked a fight for no reason. Then they pretended to be sorry. Then, they murdered the giants by tricking them.

Except this time, they couldn't get away with it because the giant's son came looking for his parents, realized what had happened, and was going to kill the dwarves himself. But they made a deal with him – they said they would give him all of the mead of poetry if he would let them live. Now, Suttung (Soo-toong) the giant knew how valuable god blood was, so he agreed. He took all three barrels back to his home inside a mountain in Jotunheim. He then hid it deep inside a hole in the mountain and told his daughter Gunnlod (Gwin-lorth) to guard it day and night.

However, there was a problem, as there usually is in these cases. That problem was Suttung's mouth. He would not keep quiet about the treasure he had, so practically everyone knew what had happened.

When news reached Asgard, all the gods including Odin also knew what had happened. They were upset that Kvasir had been murdered and they were upset that a frost giant had taken his magic blood juice to Jotunheim. But what could they do?

Odin knew this was his moment. Not only would he have an adventure, but he would also get to teach the giants a lesson, and he would be able to drink some of the mead and learn many things.

He disguised himself as a giant named Bolverk (Bowl-verkh), and off he went. He walked for a long time, and after he got to Jotunheim he walked some more. Everything was rocky and gray to look at, so he walked faster to get away from such a boring view. Soon, he came to a place near the mountains that made him think he had found the right place. The place was green and was being cared for by nine greedy human men.

They were cutting the grass with their scythes. Scythes are long knives which curve in a half circle. Since tractors and lawnmowers would not be invented for a long, long time, people used to use scythes to cut the grass or wheat stalks, or prune small tree branches. But the scythes these nine men were using were not what they were supposed to be.

What were they supposed to be, you ask? Sharp. They were supposed to be sharp. Have you ever tried cutting a tomato or a stalk of celery with a blunt knife? You have to press down harder on the tomato, and saw the knife back and forth before you can manage to even cut through it. Also, once you've cut through it, the more force you've used means the squishier the vegetable is.

This is what had happened to the scythes, and the nine greedy men were tired, sweaty, and irritated.

Odin knew these men were mean and greedy and wouldn't help him if he asked, so instead he asked them if they wanted help. They looked at him suspiciously, and asked what kind of help he could offer.

He took a whetstone out of his pocket and said he would sharpen their knives for them if they liked. A whetstone is a rock – which was part of a giant's forehead – that is often used to sharpen knives. The men looked at each other. They weren't sure if this old giant would be able to help or not, but they were interested in seeing how the whetstone worked. If it worked, they would ask him for the stone. If he refused to give it to them, they would simply kill him and take the stone for themselves. You and I are better behaved, clearly. If someone says no, we know they have a good reason for saying no. And if a god says no, they have a *very* good reason for saying no!

Finally, one of them said okay and gave Odin his scythe. Odin sat down and carefully sharpened the scythe before giving it back to him. The man took his scythes and started swinging them at the grass. The scythe went through the tough grass like a hot knife through butter. All the men were impressed and they immediately wanted Odin to sharpen their knives, too.

They asked him if they could have the whetstone, and Odin knew what would happen if he said no. Instead, he said, "sure; the one who catches it, can have it all to themselves." As he said that, he threw the stone high up into the air and moved out of the way.

The men were so eager to be the first ones to get the stone that they tried to shove each other aside to catch it. They forgot they were all still holding their scythes, so when they shoved each other aside, they stabbed each other to death.

Odin picked up his whetstone, put it back in his bag and walked down the road until a few days later he got to Baugi's home. Baugi (Bi-yee) was Suttung's brother, and Odin knew he would know where Suttung kept the mead.

Odin introduced himself as Bolverk and asked if he could spend the night in a barn. Baugi said, "Alright, but you'll have to take care of yourself and your luggage." Odin as Bolverk said, "That's not a problem. But you look upset. Is something wrong?"

"Oh, you bet something's wrong," said Baugi. "Someone murdered my nine slaves and now I've got no one to help me cut the hay."

"I could do it for you, for a price," offered Odin.

"You? You look quite scrawny for a giant," Baugi laughed.

"Yes, but looks aren't everything," said Odin. "I can do a lot of work in very little time."

"Okay, and what do you want for doing all the work?" Baugi asked.

"Just one sip of the mead of poetry your brother has." Replied Odin

"Sure", said Baugi. "If you finish cutting all the hay and stacking it neatly, I'll try and convince my brother to let both of us have a sip of the mead." *But,* he secretly thought to himself, *there's no way he can finish all of that work on his own. And even if he does, there's no way my brother or my niece will let him anywhere near the mead.*

All through summer, Odin stayed with Baugi, and worked and worked and worked as hard as nine men. When summer was over and winter started, he went to Baugi and said, "Well, I've kept my end of the deal. All the hay is cut and stacked neatly and now that summer is over, nothing is growing anymore. Let's go talk to Suttung."

Baugi was impressed by Odin, but was scared of his brother. However, he had to keep his promise, and so off they went to go talk to Suttung.

Once they arrived, he introduced Odin to his brother. "Hey Suttung, this is my friend Bolverk. He helped me all summer cutting the hay and asked for a sip of Kvasir's mead as payment."

"WHAT!?" roared Suttung. "How dare you!"

"B..b..but," Baugi stuttered.

"NEVER!" cried Suttung. "Not a single drop will I ever give ANYBODY! Now, get out!" and he stormed out of the room.

"Well," said Odin, once he and Baugi were alone, "I hope you aren't going to agree with him? Tell you what, why don't we try to steal some of it for ourselves?"

Baugi hated looking like a fool in front of other people, so he agreed.

"But we'll have to make a careful plan, Bolverk," Baugi told him. "You do know where it is hidden, right? Deep in the heart of the mountain, and it is guarded by my niece!"

"No problem," replied Odin. And from his bag, he pulled out a drill called Rati. "See this drill? It can drill through any rock as easily as if you were pushing your finger through pudding!" Saying that, he handed the drill to Baugi.

But Baugi was feeling lazy. So, he drilled through the stone for a minute or two and stopped. "There!" he shouted. "I've finished drilling through."

Odin knew he hadn't, but he pretended to believe him. He put his mouth over the opening and blew into it. Bits of stone and lots of dust flew into his mouth. He spat it out, and looked at Baugi and waited patiently.

"Fine." Baugi rolled his eyes, put the drill to the stone, and drilled some more. He felt the rock give way, so he turned to Odin and said, "I've done it! This time I really have got through!"

Once again, Odin blew into the hole and this time, the dust and bits flew out the other side. Baugi frowned at the size of the hole and said, "Wait a minute, how do we get through this? It's much too small!"

"Not for me!" said Odin. He quickly shapeshifted into a snake and slithered through the hole. By the time Baugi realized he had been tricked, Odin was halfway through to the other side. When he slithered out of the hole, he found Gunnlod, Suttung's daughter, lounging on a stool. He quickly turned back into Odin the god and as soon as Gunnlod saw his godly form, she got a huge crush on him. Odin was supposed to be quite handsome after all, and Gunnlod had had no one to talk to because her father had made sure she did nothing except guard the mead.

They spent three days and three nights getting to know each other, laughing over what they thought were good jokes, but weren't that good at all. At the end of the third day Odin told Gunnlod that he had to get back home before his friends and family came looking for him. She wanted Odin to remember her, so she asked him what he wanted. Odin said, "Do you think it would be okay for me to have three sips of the mead of poetry?"

Gunnlod didn't care about the mead; she cared about her friend and lover, Odin. *Besides,* she thought. *He just wants three sips.* "Sure," she replied and showed him where the three barrels were.

Odin picked up the first barrel and drank all of it down in one gulp.

Oh, thought Gunnlod.

Odin then picked up the second barrel and drank all of that down in one gulp.

Oh dear, she thought again.

Odin picked up the third and last barrel and drank all of that in one big gulp.

Oh no, thought Gunnlod, *If he keeps drinking that quickly, he'll get a stomach ache.* So, she told Odin that.

Odin grinned at her, "Don't worry about it babe, I'll be fine. Gotta go now before your dad catches me."

Gunnlod smiled and wished him luck. Odin transformed into an eagle and flew out of the mountain.

In the meantime, Suttung realized what had happened. How? Baugi probably told him. As soon as he saw the eagle, he knew it was Odin. So, he shape-shifted into an eagle as well and raced off after Odin. But Odin the Eagle was faster, and he flew out of Jotunheim, over Midgard, and was back home in Asgard before Suttung could catch up with him.

Once he was back in Asgard, he got three barrels and vomited the mead of poetry into them. And that's what the mead of poetry is. Kvasir's blood, Odin's vomit, and a little dash of honey.

EWWWWW! Right?

Anyway, Once he was back in Asgard, Odin took a proper drink of the mead and now he knew poetry, he had wisdom, and he knew many, many smart things. The gods were sad at having lost their friend Kvasir, but they were happy they had managed to get his blood back from the giants.

Odin, unlike Suttung and the dwarves, was generous. He shared the mead with the gods who wanted a drink of it, and occasionally he would share some with the nicest humans who wanted to become poets and writers and so on, and that's how some of the books we love best came into existence.

However, I told you we would get more gross than you could imagine, didn't I?

Some people believe that as Odin flew away from Jotunheim while Suttung was chasing him, he pooped some of the mead out as he was flying over Midgard. It didn't look like poop, so some people picked it up and ATE IT.

EW! EW! EW! EW! EW!

Any person who ate Kvasir-juice-Odin-Eagle-poop went on to write bad poetry or terrible stories that not many people like (Skjalden, 2018). Now that you've read this story, what do you think I've had? A sip of Kvasir-juice? Or Odin-eagle poo? I hope it's not the latter!

CHAPTER 6: GODLY ADVENTURES

All of the gods, whether Vanir or Aesir, would grow bored just sitting at home. Instead of reading a book, or going out to play basketball, they would go off on adventures which usually ended with either them getting hurt, or giants getting killed. I suppose that was their version of playing basketball.

ODIN IS STUCK TO THE TREE

After his adventure in Jotunheim, Odin wandered around learning more and more things. He even went to visit the Norns. When he visited them, he discovered they knew a form of magic he didn't. It was called rune magic. He wanted to learn it, but the Norns told him he couldn't learn it unless he wanted it so much he was willing to give up something very dear to him.

Odin didn't like not knowing things. He asked them what he should give up, and they said that he had to figure that out all on his own. Don't you hate it when people tell you that? Well, Odin did too. So, he sat for a while trying to think of all the things he could give up, but he couldn't think of one single thing that was important enough to sacrifice.

The other gods tried to distract him by telling stories and throwing fun parties where everyone was laughing and talking. Odin, however, was quiet.

He really, *really* didn't like not knowing things - he wanted to know it all. He wanted to know how to do Rune Magic. He wanted to understand the cycle of Ragnarok. He wanted to know what a video was. As soon as he got back to his house in Asgard, he sent his crows Huginn (Hoo-nin) and Muninn (Moo-nin) out, so they could search for an explanation and then give him an answer.

Odin was strange that way. He wanted knowledge the way you want a nice, big slice of chocolate cake with ice cream after eating a dinner you don't like. In fact, he wanted knowledge *even more* than that.

As he waited for Huginn and Muninn to get back, he decided to make a list of the things he could give up. Could he give up the mead of poetry? No, it wasn't only his, so he couldn't give that up. Could he give his magic away? No, then he wouldn't be able to help others. On and on he thought, but nothing occurred to him. When Huginn and Muninn got home, they didn't have any answers for him either.

He decided to make himself a nice hot drink of Kvasir juice and take a nap. A nap is always nice, and sometimes it helps you understand what you have to do, he thought. So, he took a nap.

As he was sleeping, the answer suddenly came to his mind and bolted upright in bed. Oh no. Oh no, no, no. Now he wished he could have slept a while longer without knowing the answer, because the answer hurt. Just like he was going to hurt.

He didn't want to tell anyone. He walked sadly from one end of Asgard to the other end of Asgard. He smiled sadly whenever people told funny jokes. He even ate his food sadly and one night the food was so good every single god except Odin was happy.

Finally, the others couldn't take it anymore. They poked at him, they talked to him, and they asked him and asked him and asked him till they were all asked out. Odin sighed sadly, and told them what was troubling him.

Once they heard what he had to say, they were horrified. "No. Don't do it!" said one. "It's not worth it."

"No. You can not do it," said another, "It will hurt and hurt and hurt."

"No. You shouldn't do it," said yet another god. "It won't mean anything."

Odin replied sadly but grandly, "It will mean everything, because knowledge is always worth having. Even when it hurts."

Now the gods were sad too. Odin knew that the only sacrifice that would be acceptable would be his own death. It was why very, very, *very* few gods and goddesses knew Rune magic. But Odin being Odin, he had a plan.

First he told all the gods and goddesses not to help him. Then he told No-Name Eagle, Ratatoskr the lying squirrel, the goats, the stag, and the deer not to help him or feed him.

Then he took a deep breath and climbed Yggdrasil till he reached a high branch from where he could look down and see the Well of Urd. He took a rope and hung himself, and then took a spear and speared himself with it on to The World Tree like a human or godly fly pinned by a dart.

Don't try this at home, kids! In fact, DON'T DARE TRY THIS AT ALL. If you want to hang something, hang a photograph on a wall.

Where were we? Ah yes. Odin was being a pinned fly.

He hung on Yggdrasil for nine whole days and for nine whole nights, and afterward he was still alive, looking down into the Well of Urd. The Well of Urd looked back at him. The water in the well was so clear and still, it looked like a mirror or a screen. The well considered whether to reveal the secret of Rune magic to Odin and decided to wait the full nine days to see if he was serious.

If you ask me, the fact that he stuck himself with a spear as though he were a kebab, would prove he's pretty serious. But what do I know? I'm not an all-knowing well of fate.

So for nine days and nine nights Odin looked at the well, The Well looked at Odin, and all the gods and the animals living in the tree looked at them looking at each other. As the days went by, the well first showed him nine magical songs and waited to see if he would leave. But Odin was stubborn. He wanted to learn the runes, so he stayed on the tree.

Next, the well showed him nine words of stupendous power. The well was sure Odin would leave now. Clearly, the well didn't know everything, because Odin stayed there stuck to the tree. Oh erm...you know what I mean. He didn't go anywhere.

The Well of Urd was impressed. So, on the end of the ninth day, when Odin was almost mostly dead — 'mostly dead' is not *completely* dead, as we all know — the well decided to accept his sacrifice and show Odin the runes.

You must be wondering what runes are. Runes are the Viking or Norse alphabet and are still used today. But for the Norse gods and the Norse people, the alphabets were more than something you could use to write a word or sentence, the way I am doing right now. Each alphabet was magic and when it was placed together to form the right words, the symbols could create very powerful magic — the same way the Norns could.

When the well showed him the secret of rune magic, the spear loosened and Odin fell off the tree. Thankfully, he didn't have very far to fall and everyone else was waiting and watching, making sure he wouldn't hurt himself more than he already had.

After he recovered (gods tend to recover very quickly if they're only *mostly* dead), Odin was more knowledgeable and more powerful than any of the Aesir gods. However, Odin quickly put the rest of his plan in practice. He wasn't usually a selfish god, and he believed if people wanted to learn, then they should be able to do just that. So, after he learnt rune magic, he went and taught others who wanted to learn how to read and write the runes as well.

Finally, he thought, everything was how it was supposed to be. Now he could get on with doing god-like things such as fighting battles, playing tricks, and serving justice, all of which were just human things but remember, on a godly level.

MIMIR LOSES HIS HEAD

Do you remember the story of the war between the Aesir gods and the Vanir gods? Or how Njord and his two children Frey and Freya came to live in Asgard as a truce?

Well, Odin was supposed to send people to the Vanir as well, so he chose Hoenir the handsome and Mimir the wise to live in Vanaheim with all the other Vanir.

Since Njord had gone to Asgard, the Vanir had to choose a new leader, but they didn't know whom to choose.

The Vanir didn't always make smart decisions, and since Hoenir was so handsome to look at, they thought he must be just as smart too, so they elected him to be their new leader.

This is why you don't pick people based on what they look like, because as you can guess, this story does not end well. But not for the person you would expect.

After he became the leader, Hoenir made one smart decision. He made Mimir his adviser, and that was the only smart decision he ever made. So, when the Vanir came to him to ask him for his advice, or to sort out a fight, he would turn to Mimir. Mimir would step in and answer questions, help them sort out their troubles, and generally be a very clever person.

The Vanir were happy to have such wonderful people and they thanked the Aesir for sending them to Vanaheim. For a long time, that was how things worked. Mimir would be happy to use his wisdom, and Hoenir would be happy to look at himself in the mirror or have people admire him.

Then one day, when Hoenir was admiring his new cape and

brushing his beautiful hair, some of the important Vanir came rushing into the room. There was an emergency and they desperately needed Hoenir to tell them what they should do.

Hoenir began to panic; he knew there was no way he would be able to give them intelligent advice. He tried to stall the Vanir while he searched for Mimir. But he couldn't find Mimir anywhere, because Mimir was taking a break away from everything. Without Mimir telling him what to do or say, Hoenir could barely open his mouth.

The Vanir couldn't understand why he wasn't saying anything the way he usually did. They asked him again and again, until he finally began to talk. Once he began to say something, the Vanir grew more and more horrified and started to wish he would stop talking.

Do you know people like that? When they start talking, they talk and talk and talk but they have nothing intelligent to say? And then because they don't stop talking, you become angry? That is exactly how the Vanir were feeling. They began to feel as though the Aesir had cheated them by giving them Hoenir and Mimir in exchange for Njord, Frey, and Freya. They were so angry, they thought perhaps Mimir wasn't as smart as he was either. And since Mimir wasn't as pretty to look at as Hoenir was, they thought it was better to get rid of Mimir instead of Hoenir. So, when Mimir got back from his picnic and before he had a chance to open his mouth to even say hello, they cut off his head, packed it up neatly in a box, and sent it as a surprise package to Odin.

Odin was relaxing at home with everyone else when the package arrived. Njord also came to look at what the Vanir had sent. Perhaps they had sent something nice for him, too, to remind him of home. You and I know they had not!

Odin opened the package and everyone standing around it gasped in horror. Odin was upset, Njord was angry, and everyone else was shocked. Njord wanted to go punish his people for doing something so terrible, but before anyone could tell Odin anything,

Odin began to work some magic. After all, he didn't stick himself to The World Tree with his spear for nothing. One of the magical songs that The Well of Urd had taught him, was how to give the gift of speech and thought back to someone who had died.

Odin picked up Mimir's head and started singing to it. The song echoed around the hall and everyone stopped to listen. Even Njord calmed down long enough to listen and smile. Once Odin had finished his song, he reached into his pocket and took out some special lotion and rubbed into and over it, so that it wouldn't grow moldy and gross.

Then Mimir opened his eyes, looked around at everyone and smiled. His head now looked like one of those head statues you see in a museum, except it was alive and talking. But he no longer wanted to answer any questions from anyone else except Odin, because Odin had brought him back. Who knew what someone else would cut off if they became angry with him?

The other gods wanted to know what to do about the Vanir. Should they not be punished for doing something so horrible, especially to someone who did not deserve it even a little bit? "Well, yes," said Odin. "And I've thought of the perfect punishment."

"What is it?" said Nord. "Shall I make the waves of the sea rise up and swallow them?"

"What is it?" said Thor. "Shall I go and beat them all up?"

"What is it?" asked Skadi. "Shall I go turn everything into ice?"

"No," Odin said. "We shall let Hoenir continue to stay there and rule them. He talks too much and says so many stupid things, so that will be punishment enough."

CHAPTER 7: MORE GODLY ADVENTURES

T he Gods do seem pretty quarrelsome, don't they? It seems as though every story we read is one in which the gods are picking fights with each other, or simply *waiting* to pick a fight with each other.

The gods knew this was a problem. They knew not everything could be solved by picking a fight, or with magic. But how would they sort out this problem? Well, one day the answer came to them. Literally. And it arrived in the form of a person.

THE OTHER GOD OF POETRY

Do you remember Gunnlod? The giantess who guarded the mead of poetry and then gave it to Odin to drink? Well, she and Odin had a son whom Odin didn't know about. Gunnlod named him Bragi (Bra-yee) because even though he knew how to fight, he liked to bring peace instead by having fun conversations. He wanted to talk about things, help people, write stories and poems, solve problems, and help people think for themselves so they could do the right thing.

Unfortunately, in a place like Jotunheim, all the giants thought he was a wuss. Why, they wondered, would anyone sit around and come up with stories, when they could fight? Gunnlod knew the giants wouldn't appreciate her son's talents and they might even try to kill him. So, she called him, and told him she was sending him to his father, Odin, and to be a good boy when he got there.

Bragi was excited to get to know his father, so he hugged Gunnlod and set off for Asgard. When he arrived there, the gods were in the middle of a deep discussion on how to stop themselves and humans and everyone else from picking useless fights that would lead to war.

Bragi walked up to Odin and explained who he was and asked if he could help in any kind of way. Odin was happy to meet his son, and pestered him for news about Gunnlod. When Bragi had convinced Odin that Gunnlod was happy and fine on her own, he once again offered to help the gods solve their problem.

"But it could be really dangerous, son," protested Odin. "Your mum may not want you to do this."

"Some people talk too much while others talk too little, and even *that* causes them to fight," sighed Frigg. "Are you sure you want to do this?"

"I like talking to people and helping them with their problems," Bragi answered. "Sometimes, if they don't want to listen to advice, they will agree to listen to stories – and I'm pretty good at making advice sound like fun stories, writing your hero moments so that others will remember, and just stories in general."

"Hm. I don't know," Odin said worriedly.

"Come on, dad. Mum won't worry because she knows I can fight, but she also knows I like to try every possible peaceful solution first, before I kick someone's butt!"

"Okay, you've convinced me." Odin continued. "Tonight, we will hold a party to welcome you properly and then you can start to do what you do best. How does that sound?"

"Awesome!" replied Bragi excitedly.

That night everyone gathered for a party that had everything - streamers, fireworks, and delicious food that was so good it made you cry happy tears, along with games and music.

In the middle of the party, Frey wandered up to Bragi, slung an arm around him and took him around the room introducing him to everyone. When they stopped in front of Idunn (Ee-thoon), the goddess of youth, she blushed while Bragi, who was never at a loss for words, stammered out a "H…h…hi."

Oho! thought Frey. *They like each other. How cute! I should try and help them.*

Just then, the musicians stopped playing to take a little break. Frey had an idea.

"Hey, Bragi. I heard you know how to sing? Why don't you sing something for us, huh? I'm sure we'd all like to listen – especially Idunn. She loves music."

"Oh no, I couldn't," said Bragi

"Please. I'd love to hear you sing," said Idunn shyly. Frey hid a grin. His plan was working!

"Okay, but you have to promise not to laugh if I get it wrong," he said, smiling at Idunn. Then he began to sing.

As he sang the entire party fell silent. The fireworks stopped fireworking, the streamers stopped streaming, and even Yggdrasill didn't move a leaf. Bragi's voice was beautiful. Imagine the most beautiful music you've ever heard in your life, and it *still* would not compare to how wonderful Bragi's voice was.

When he finished singing, Bragi looked around. Everyone was either smiling, or happy-crying, or smiling and happy-crying, while Idunn looked at him as though she wanted to give him all the apples of youth from her garden. This time, Bragi blushed.

Then Frey quickly told them to go take a walk together before everyone else decided to come and talk to Bragi.

"Freeeyyyy!" whined Thjalfi (Th-yal-way), Thor's human servant, "Why did you send him away? I wanted to talk to him."

"I wanted to talk to him as well," Frigg protested.

"None of you are looking at the larger picture," said Frey, rolling his eyes. "Bragi likes Idunn, Idunn likes Bragi, and if they fall in love and get married, Bragi will be one of us forever."

"Oohhh, I like that!" said Freya.

"You sure do some quick thinking, Frey," said Odin. "I do too. Quick thinking, I mean. I thought we should make him the official singer of the royal court and the god of poetry and knowledge."

"Ooh! Yes!" the gods said in unison.

"While no one can replace Kvasir – may I rest his soul – Bragi seems just as kind and smart and therefore is more than qualified. We should start planning the whole thing!" said Odin. Then he began to make a list.

And it happened exactly the way they had hoped. Bragi and

Idunn fell in love and got married. Odin made Bragi the god of poetry and knowledge and gave him the right to travel through all the worlds without needing a godly passport. As a wedding gift, Idunn, who also knew rune magic, carved runes onto Bragi's tongue to make his speech skills even more excellent than they already were.

I mean, I would have settled for some cake, but to each their own.

HOW LOKI BUILT A WALL AND ODIN GOT A SPIDER HORSE

Do you remember reading about the war between the Aesir and the Vanir? How could you forget. It seems as though everything started there, instead of when Odin, Vile, and Ve created the world, doesn't it?

This story is also set a little while after the Aesir and Vanir war. After the war, and after Hoenir and Mimir had gone to Vanaheim while Njord, Frey, and Freya had settled in Asgard, everyone was a little worried. Why was everyone worried? Because even though the war was over, they were anxious that someone might try to invade or attack them again.

Odin walked around Asgard while the other gods trailed after him. Everyone looked around and they knew they needed something, but what? What would help?

Thor looked around and saw wide, lush green grasslands, and just beyond that he could see the other worlds, too. But if he could see the other worlds, that meant they could see them as well! Maybe they needed to put up curtains, thought Thor.

Sif looked all around and saw wheat fields which would soon be ready for cutting. She was the goddess of autumn and of the harvest, so she noticed stuff like that. She could see the wheat fields of Midgard, and the no-wheat, no-field land of Jotunheim. But if she could see all of those lands, then it was possible they could see all that was in Asgard, too. Perhaps, they needed to grow giant fields of wheat around the edges of Asgard.

"I know what we need," said Odin decisively. "What we need is what Vile, Ve, and I made in Midgard."

"Humans?" asked Freya.

"No. Walls."

"How will no walls help?" asked Tyr (Teer).

"Ugh, I meant, no, we don't need humans. I meant we need walls," huffed Odin irritably.

"Ohhh, that makes more sense," said Tyr. "But didn't you already use all of Ymir's eyebrows to make the walls around Midgard?"

"Yes. And my magic isn't strong enough to build a wall which will keep out the frost giants, and who knows what else."

"Then what are we going to do?" asked Heimdall (Hime-dal).

"We'll have to hire someone. Let's go back to the house and make a list of all the people we know who can do this." said Odin. So they all traipsed back to Odin's mansion. As they were making their list, which really was just a blank piece of paper because they couldn't think of even one person, a stranger wandered into Asgard.

"Who are you and what do you want?" asked Frigg.

"I am the best builder in this whole universe. In fact, I'm so much the best, you can call me the Master Builder."

"Why should we believe you are as good as you say you are?"

"Because I can build you a wall," smirked the stranger. Odin and all the gods sat up straight when they heard that.

"Anyone can build a wall," sniffed Odin dismissively.

"Not like my wall, they can't," the stranger boasted.

"Oh? Tell us what makes your wall so special, then," Odin said, trying to play it cool.

"My wall will be made of stones so large and thick that the wall itself will be so tall and thick that no one – even the frost giants – will be able to break it down. And I'll do it in a year and a half, not a day more," boasted the stranger. "Of course, I make no promises that it can stand against anyone when Ragnarok arrives," he added hastily.

"Of course, of course. Ragnarok is a different matter altogether," agreed Odin. "And if you manage to build this wall, what do you want as payment? Gold? More gold? A medal made of gold?"

"I don't want gold at all, thanks," said the stranger.

"What do you want, then?" asked Loki. He was immediately suspicious, because he knew how people played tricks. He was the god of mischief and tricks, after all.

"Three things. One, I want the sun. Two, I want the moon. And three, and most importantly, I want Freya to be my wife."

"Anything else? Would you like us to give you the throne of Asgard, and the mead of poetry too?" Odin drawled sarcastically.

"Nope, just the three things I mentioned," the stranger said.

Freya stamped her foot. "I AM NOT A *THING!* HOW DARE YOU!" she yelled.

"Okay, I think we need to discuss this privately. Can you wait outside please?" asked Loki.

" Sure," the stranger replied, leaving to wait outside the hall.

"What do you mean, discuss?" asked Frey. "There's nothing to discuss! We'll find another way to build the wall, but we are not giving my sister to whoever that person says he is."

"He said he was the master builder. Weren't you listening?" asked Loki.

"I don't care who he says he is," yelled Freya. "I am not marrying him!"

"And *I* am not giving up Sol and Mani to whatever he says he is," said Baldr (Bal-door), the god of light.

"No, of course you aren't marrying him, Freya, and no we're not giving up the Sun and the Moon either, Baldr," Loki said soothingly.

"What I meant was, how about we let him think he's going to get all that he asked for, but we trick him so he ends up building the wall for free and we keep Freya and Sol and Mani?"

"Sounds like a recipe for disaster, but I like that plan," Odin nodded.

"Well, I don't!" said Freya crossly. "It's not your freedom that is being discussed here! You marry him if you feel that strongly about it."

Baldr wasn't very pleased either, but he tried to be fair. "Okay, explain your plan and then we'll see."

"Simple. We make it harder. Instead of a year and a half, we give him only six months, no help from anyone, and when he can't finish it, he doesn't get anything or anyone."

All the gods considered Loki's plan. Given how impossible it was to build a wall in that short a time, it did sound like a good plan to everyone except Sol, Mani, Baldr, Freya, and Frey. They called the stranger back into the hall, and told him since he was such a fantastic builder and everything, they were sure he could do it in less than half the time.

He frowned and hesitated.

Loki came forward with a smile and put his hand on the stranger's shoulder. Look, MB...can I call you MB? You know, short form for Master Builder?"

The stranger shrugged.

Loki went on sweetly, "Look, MB, we're offering you a pretty good deal. You work for six months, and you get the Sun and her chariot of pure Muspel-ien Gold, the Moon and his chariot of Muspel-ien silver, and Freya herself, the goddess of love and beauty and all that awesome stuff! You'll be the envy of every single person in the universe. All we're asking is for you to complete the work in six months. If you don't, you get nothing, but if you do, you get everything you wanted! Do we have a deal?"

MB thought about Loki's words and said, "Hm. Okay, but I have conditions of my own."

"Alright, let's hear them."

"I want my horse Svadifari (Sva-thil-fa-ree) to help me." MB folded his arms across his wide chest and stared at all the gods.

"Your horse?" asked Loki.

"Yes," nodded MB.

"You want your horse to help you build a wall?" asked Odin disbelievingly.

"Yes, I do." MB nodded harder.

Loki shook his head with barely hidden amusement and asked, "Okay, what else?"

"That's it," MB said.

"That's it?" the gods asked together.

"Yeah," he replied, wondering why they needed to have everything repeated.

"Sure! We can agree to that. All the best!" said Loki, as Odin and MB shook hands.

What a fool MB is, thought Loki. *He isn't just going to be fun to trick; he is going to be easy to trick too!*

MB started work immediately. As soon as he did, the sky grew stormy and it grew cold and every single person who didn't have to be outside, was sitting inside their house by the fireside drinking some nice hot cocoa.

The storm was, of course, the work of the gods, who were planning to keep the weather horrid and uncomfortable so MB wouldn't be able to finish his work on time. But MB surprised them.

He marched off to the mountains, and piled twenty boulders on to his cart. Each boulder was the size of three grownups standing on top of each other and was just as wide too. The gods were standing in a tower and watching him pile boulder after boulder onto the cart and they laughed and went downstairs. No horse was going to be able to pull that cart on his own. The gods were safe. Or so they thought.

As soon as MB had finished piling the boulders onto the cart, Svadilfari pulled the cart as though there were nothing but feathers in it. The next day, there was already a circle of stone halfway round Asgard. The gods were shocked, and so this time they kept a close watch.

As they monitored his progress, MB finished the first line of stones around Agard. It wasn't a wall; instead it looked as though MB had made a circle bench all around Asgard. Once MB had finished with the first line, he didn't stop for a sandwich or a soda, or a... well, whatever the gods ate back in the day, and went off to the mountain once more. This time the gods were waiting to see how he was able to do this, and they saw how his horse pulled the cart with the boulders in it. Their worry began to grow again.

MB was working day and night. Or rather, MB and his horse were working day and night. They worked through bad weather and good weather and just weather, but they didn't stop – even for half a minute.

As MB built the wall, he stacked the stones together the way you used to play with building blocks. He kept working and the wall got closer and closer to completion while Freya grew closer and closer to sending Loki out to be used as building material for the wall as well.

Finally, the sixth month arrived and every day of that last month, the wall grew a little stronger and higher and the panic inside the room of the gods also grew stronger and higher. What could they do? By this time Freya was planning how to make Loki suffer, Baldr was planning to kick Loki like a football, and Loki was planning on running away and hiding.

Apart from that, not one of them had an actual plan.

"Loki, what have you done?" thundered Odin.

"Me?" squeaked Loki.

"You've ruined everything!" roared Heimdall.

"Me?" yelped Loki.

"Find a way to fix this, or I'll throw my hammer at you!" growled Thor, as he gripped his hammer tightly.

"Of course, I'll fix this, it's all part of my plan! Why does no one trust me?" asked Loki sadly.

"LOKI!" yelled all the gods in unison.

"Alright, I'm going! But you'd all better have a party ready for me when I get back from saving all of you," he called over his shoulder as he sauntered out of the door.

As soon as he was outside and no one could see, he leaned against a wall and wiped the sweat from his forehead with a soft "Phew!" Then, he walked near to where MB was working and hid himself so he could spy on him and come up with a plan.

"Why did I think he would be easy to trick? Now I have to figure something out and I have no idea what, so I can make sure the others aren't mad at me. Argh. Think brain, think!" He thought hard and long, but quickly since he didn't have much time.

Loki wasn't a nice god, but he wasn't a mean god at first. In the beginning and during the middle, he really didn't want anything bad to happen to the others. He just found it funny when they got in trouble usually because of him, but he liked getting them out of trouble, too. It was only towards the end that he let his jealousy grow so much, that his anger turned into hate, and he turned into the meanest, most horrid god ever.

This story happened around the beginning, so while everyone would get irritated with him, they still sort of liked him and he still liked them. Which was why he was trying to come up with a plan to get Freya and the others out of this mess. As he watched MB and Svadilfari the horse work, he got an idea. He thought it was such a good idea he almost did a little dance, but stopped himself just in time. He knew he would have to wait for the darkness of night, to make sure his idea had the best chance of succeeding. He then walked off deep into the forest.

That night as MB headed to the mountain to get more boulders, Svadilfari trotted next to him not even a bit out of breath from the day's work. Suddenly Svadilfari heard a noise and his ears twitched; the noise came again and since he was curious, he turned his head to look. There at the edge of the forest was a black mare – a female horse.

Svadilfari's breath caught in his throat. This mare was the loveliest mare he had ever seen. She looked as though she were made out of starlight and a piece of night sky. He wanted to get to know her.

Just as he thought that, the mare turned away and ran into the forest. Svadilfari was already halfway in love with the mare, so instead of staying and helping MB with the boulders, he chased after the mare into the forest.

MB ran after him, shouting at him and telling him to stop, but Svadilfari didn't listen. The only thing he was listening to was the sound of the mare's hooves as she ran fast. So he ran faster. He ran so fast that MB couldn't keep up.

MB was in despair; his horse had disappeared and so had his chance of completing the wall in time. There was only a little bit left, but that bit still required more boulders than he could carry.

He tried, but he couldn't do it. His horse hadn't come back, and he wasn't able to finish the wall.

At the end of the sixth month, he went to meet Odin and all the other gods. "I've completed most of the wall," He told them.

"The agreement was for all of the wall, or nothing," Odin reminded him.

"Yes, I know. I am willing to give up the Sun and the Moon as payment, but I want Freya."

"And we wanted the wall completed on time, but we don't always get what we want, do we?" smirked Freya.

MB looked at all the gods and grew angry. "I know you've tricked me somehow, so you'd better give me part of my payment."

Frey looked around and said in a fake innocent tone, "Trick you? How would we do that? Do any of us look like we know how to play tricks?"

MB grew so angry that first he grew purple in the face, and then he grew and grew and grew until his real self was revealed. He was a frost giant in disguise! He tried to grab Freya, but before Freya could kick him and set her cats on him, Thor grabbed his hammer and struck him over the head with it.

He hit him so hard that MB's skull shattered and turned into pebbles all over the world and the gods all cheered and began to plan a party. Odin stopped them. "We have to plan a party for Thor for killing MB of course, but where is Loki? I'm sure he tricked the giant, but how?"

Everyone looked around and felt a little bad. Only a very little, since some of them were still irritated with him.

"How about we plan the party now, and then have the party once he gets back?" suggested Baldr.

"Good idea. Till then let's not worry about him too much," said Freya.

Everyone agreed and went back home to do what they usually do.

A couple of months later, Loki walked into the throne room calling out cheerily to everyone. But he had someone with him. A young horse with a shiny silvery coat, and eight legs! It had four legs in front and four legs at the back, and it walked as though it was going to start running at any minute. *Was it a horse, a spider, or an octopus?* wondered some of the gods.

Odin was just as surprised, but he was also pleased to see Loki. "Where have you been all this time? We were beginning to worry that you were either in trouble or that you were being trouble," he teased.

"Har Har, you think you're so funny," sniffed Loki. Then he grinned and said, "But enough of that; let me introduce you to my son, Sleipnir (Sleyp-neer), the eight-legged horse who can fly, walk and run on water, and run faster than any horse ever."

"*WHAT?*" yelled everyone in surprise.

"I was the black mare. How else do you think I distracted MB's horse, Svaldilfari? With sugar cubes?" asked Loki scornfully.

"You tricky trickster!" said Freya admiringly.

"You sneaky little shapeshifter," laughed Thor.

Loki laughed. He liked being admired for his brains and his cunning. He gave Sleipnir to Odin as a gift, and then all of them got on with the serious business of partying the night away.

CHAPTER 8: THE OTHER TWO STRONGEST GODS

We all know how smart and cunning Odin is, but many people believe Thor and Frey were and are Odin's equal. It is a little unfortunate that Thor is now shown as a bit of a dumb god who only like fighting and drinking, while some of the people who have read about Frey like to dismiss him as a god who was a fool.

The truth is Thor was smart and clever when he needed to be, and Frey was quick-witted and a strong warrior when he needed to be. And they were both very loyal to the people they loved, as we will see in these stories.

WHY THOR GETS HEADACHES

Thor's problems start, as they usually do, when he ends up fighting someone because of someone else. This is what happened when Odin decided to go off on a little adventure on his own, to Jotunheim (*Thor's Duel with Hrungnir - Norse Sagas - Norse Mythology*, 2017).

Now, if you and I dislike someone, we don't visit their house, because we don't want to end up picking a quarrel with them. When Odin is in one of his moods, on the other hand, he likes nothing better than picking quarrels.

So there Odin was, riding Sleipnir and talking to him the way we do to our dogs and cats, except Sleipnir understood Odin and Odin understood Sleipnir. As he was riding through the mountains and looking at all the rocks and ice, he came to the edge of a deep crater. It looked like a bottomless pit, but since there was a bridge, Odin didn't really care much about the pit. He and Sleipnir moved to the bridge to cross it.

See, if I had a magic, eight-legged horse that could walk on water, or fly through the sky, I would've just flown over the bridge. But that is me. And if Odin had done that, we would not have had a story. Also, perhaps Sleipnir was tired, or grumpy, and he just did not want to fly. Either way, they decide to walk over the bridge instead of flying over the pit.

In front of the bridge was a large boulder - much, much larger than the ones MB used to build the wall around Asgard, which is one of the reasons Odin didn't really trust boulders. In this case, he was right not to trust it, because as he stood in front of it, the boulder moved. It moved and stretched and stood tall, and Odin sat on his horse and sighed and thought resignedly, *Here we go again.*

The rock giant grumbled, "Who are you and what are you doing here?"

For a minute Odin was surprised and a little insulted. How many people did this giant know who had an eight-legged horse, or had a shining spear, or looked so handsome even with only one eye? How did he not know who he was? Did he live under a rock? Or maybe he didn't know anything because he *was* a rock. Hm.

"My name is Odin, and I am the ruler of all the gods," Odin informed him. Now step aside, whoever you are, because I'd like to cross that bridge."

"My name is not 'Whoever'; my name is Hrungnir (Thoong-nir), and I am the rock god," answered the giant.

"No such thing as a rock god. You're making that up," said Odin dismissively.

"Am not!" answered Hrungnir. "I'll prove it to you; my heart and my head are made of stone."

"That doesn't prove anything about you being a god except for the fact that you've got rocks in your head," said Odin.

"Oi! Don't you talk to me like that, or the only way you'll cross this bridge is in a coffin!" said Hrungnir.

Odin looked up at him for a minute. "Alright, tell you what? We'll have a race across the bridge. Me on Sleipnir and you on your horse, and if you win you can cut my head off."

"Hahahahahaha! My horse Gullfaxi (Gool-fa-she) is a hundred times faster than your weird horse, so sure! I'll race you and win and then use your head as a bowling ball!" sneered Hrungnir.

This time Sleipnir was insulted. How dare that stinky rock call him slow! He would show him.

Hrungnir climbed onto his horse and as soon as the race started, Sleipnir was off like a bullet. Gullfaxi wasn't far behind, but Sleipnir had eight legs. He could have run twice that distance without growing tired. Hrungnir was angry; he thought he would win without a problem, but no.

But by the time he reached the end point of the race, which Odin had cleverly chosen to be Asgard, Odin had already showered and dressed and was sitting on his throne.

Since Odin had won the race, he was feeling generous. So, he invited Hrungnir into the hall the way they usually would as a guest. Then Odin invited him to stay for dinner as well.

At dinner, Hrungnir ate a wonderful dinner of chicken in rock sauce, roast ox with pebbles, and stone salad. And then Odin offered him some mead. Unfortunately, the cup the mead was poured into was Thor's cup. Nobody noticed since Thor was away visiting friends and fighting trolls. Even more unfortunately, Hrungnir would not stop drinking mead. And the more he drank, the more drunk he became.

The more drunk he became, the more he talked. But his talking wasn't the "fun conversation" sort of talking, oh no. Hrungnir's idea of small talk was to threaten people. He turned to Odin and told him, "You watch. I'm going to turn Asgard into a pile of rocks. Before I do that, I'm going to kill all of the gods, starting with you." And he pointed at Odin. Or rather, he meant to point at Odin, but he was so drunk, he ended up pointing at an empty chair instead.

Odin spoke soothingly. "Sure, Hrungnir. Sounds like a great idea, but for now why don't you put the cup down and go to bed? Let's talk about this when you're not drunk."

"Drunk? WHO ARE YOU CALLING DRUNK, YOU ONE-EYED BEETLE!?" yelled Hrungnir. "I am absolutely, completely, and totally not drunk!"

"No, he may not be drunk, but he certainly is a jerk," Freya muttered to Sif.

"Yup. And if he doesn't stop talking, Thor will return and thump him," replied Sif.

Hrungnir saw them muttering to each other and got a drunken idea which he simply had to announce. "After I've killed all of you, I'll leave Sif and Freya alive and take them with me to Jotunheim as my wives!"

"Uh Oh," Odin said.

"Oh no," Frey also said.

"WHY DO PEOPLE I DON'T KNOW KEEP WANTING TO MARRY ME?" yelled Freya. "All I want is to practice my magic and take care of my cats."

"And why do people forget who *I'm* married to?" asked Sif, annoyed.

She had a point. The goddesses of Asgard and Vanheim were as dangerous and sometimes even more so than the gods. They, like Frey and Bragi and the others, didn't fight because they didn't want to, not because they couldn't.

Anyway, while all of this yelling was going on, Hrungnir lumbered out of his chair and said, "I'm going to take them with me now, and no one can stop me, so there!"

As he moved towards them to grab them, the entire dining room heard thunder roaring outside just before the hall was flooded by a flash of lighting. When the light dimmed, Thor was standing in front of Hrungnir and hefting his hammer.

"You! Not only do you drink out of my cup when I'm not here, but you threaten to KILL MY DAD AND EVERYONE ELSE, AND THEN KIDNAP MY WIFE AND SISTER-IN-LAW? YOU'RE DEAD!"

When he saw Thor, Hrungnir got un-drunk in a hurry. "No, no, that's not what I meant at all!" he tried to lie.

"Really? What exactly did you mean, then?" snarled Thor.

Hrungnir thought since he had nothing to lose, so he might as well challenge Thor. "I meant, I'll do all of what I said, after I kill you in a proper fight. Or are you telling me you're going to be brave and fight an unarmed man who is a guest in your house?"

Thor was mad, but he realized he couldn't hurt the giant while he was a guest in his home. It would break the rules of being a good host, and for the Norse, this was an unbreakable law — except of course there were lots of people who broke it and were then punished for it.

But Thor could not break this law. He was a god and he was supposed to be a fair god most of the time.

So, he said, "Fine. I won't kill you here. Instead I will meet you in a proper fight, and we can choose where, because I won't fight you in Jotunheim, and you won't fight me in Asgard."

Hrungnir wanted to fight in Jotunheim, because that way he could cheat, but now he did not have that option. So, he said, "Okay, what about the rock field near Jotunheim?"

Thor agreed, they decided they would each pick a helper, and then decided to have their fight the next day.

Hrungnir got on his horse and raced back to Jotunheim. He got all the frost giants together and told them what had happened. Some of the giants were scared. They had met Thor before and they knew he was strong enough to fight and kill a group of giants if he was truly angry.

Some of the other giants were planning to use this fight to make the frost giants famous. After all, Hrungnir had a head and heart of stone, so he would be very difficult to kill. If he managed to kill Thor, they would be famous! But Hrungnir would need help.

Since the gods had said each of them was allowed a helper, the giants decided to make a helper for Hrungnir. They made him out of clay, but since they could not find the heart of a giant to bring him to life, they decided to use the heart of a small mare instead. They named this clay-giant "Mist-Calf".

They made him so tall his head was in the clouds, the clouds which were once Ymir's brains. They made him so wide, that his chest was almost the size of a football field. The giants were satisfied. Surely, Thor would take one look at this giant they had made, and be terrified. When the next day arrived, both of them went to the rock field to wait for Thor.

Thor had gotten ready for the battle and he had picked Thjalfi, his human servant, as his helper. Thjalfi was the fastest human runner in all the worlds, no one except Sleipnir could beat him.

He raced ahead of Thor and got to the field well before Thor reached it. He saw Hrungnir and Mist-Calf waiting, and Hrungnir was holding his whetstone and his stone shield. Mist-Calf did not have a weapon, because everyone thought his size would be enough to give him an advantage, but they forgot about the heart they had used while making him.

Thjalfi took one look at Hrungnir and started laughing, "Hah! This fight will be over before you know it! You're holding your shield out in front of you, but every single person who's fought Thor knows he'll attack you from under the ground. Of course, you can't ask anyone he's fought because they're all dead — just like you will be soon!"

Hrungnir said, "Oh yeah? We'll see about that." And promptly put his shield down and stood on top of it instead. "Let's see him try to attack me now", he smirked. Thjalfi pretended to be upset at having told him this, but inside his head he was laughing. Their plan was going well.

Barely a second later, all of them heard the sound of loud thunder and Thor flew down from the sky in a bolt of lightning. Hrungnir knew Thjalfi had tricked him so he promised himself he would deal with the human later, and he turned to face the god of thunder. As he faced Thor, Thor threw his hammer at Hrungnir's head with all his strength and at the same time Hrungnir threw his whetstone straight at Thor.

Thor's hammer flew through the air with so much force that it hit the whetstone and shattered it, flew straight through that, and hit Hrungnir in the head, shattering his head too. People say that all the whetstones in the world today are pieces of Hrungnir's original weapon.

Anyway, when Mist-Calf saw this, he was so scared he peed his pants. Thjalfi attacked Mist-Calf, cut off his legs, and when he fell over, quickly killed him. Thjalfi looked around for Thor, and all the gods who were pretty sure Thor would defeat the giant also looked around for the god of thunder.

And then Thjalfi saw him. He was pinned under Hrungnir's leg and he felt a little wooly headed. He tried to get up from under the giant, but the rock giant was much too heavy for Thor to push off. First, Thjalfi tried to help, but as nice a gesture as that was, he was only human. Then Odin tried. Then Njord tried, and one by one all the gods tried, but they couldn't lift the giant off Thor.

Then, Thor's three-year-old son, Magni, who hadn't seen all that had happened, noticed his dad couldn't move. So, he went right up to Thor and lifted the giant's leg up so Thor could crawl out from under it. At three years of age, *I* was drawing on the walls with crayons, but you should talk to your parents. Perhaps you were as strong as Magni and were able to lift very heavy things!

Thor and the other gods were so impressed, they praised him and Thor hugged Magni and told him that when he grew up, he would probably be stronger than Thor himself! Then, as a thank you present, he took Hrungnir's horse Gullfaxi and gave it to Magni to ride.

Odin was feeling a little selfish, so he said, "What will three year old Magni do with such a fancy horse? You should give it to me instead."

Thor looked at Odin in annoyance and asked, "Did you manage to lift the giant's leg off me? Don't answer that. Let's talk about why I was fighting that giant in the first place. Because I don't remember racing a rock giant and then inviting him to have dinner with us and then letting him insult and threaten everyone in the hall. Do you want me to remind you who did that?"

"I don't know what you're talking about," said Odin sulkily.

"Sure you don't," said Thor. "For now, let's go home. I have a headache."

This was curious, because Thor almost never got a headache. He was the one giving trolls and giants a headache. So Frigg looked at his temple closely and gasped. In the fight with Hrungnir, one of the pieces of the whetstone weapon had struck Thor's forehead and was now so deep in his head that it was stuck and no one, even the sorceress Groa, was able to get it out.

This is why, if you lose your temper and throw a whetstone across the room, it moves the stone in Thor's head and gives him really terrible headaches, which makes him so mad that he creates storms of thunder and lightning. Is it stormy where you are right now? Are you sure you didn't throw a whetstone across the room?

HOW FREY GOT A STAG'S HEAD

Frey was bored. Have you noticed how trouble often starts because gods are bored? It was no different this time. Since Frey was bored, he wandered all around Vanaheim. Then he went to visit the gods in Asgard, but his dad Njord and his stepmom Skadi were away.

Freya was busy practicing her sword fighting skills with Sif in an open carriage drawn by her cats, Thor was away smashing some giant's head in, and Odin and Frigg were off on a date. Everyone was busy and Frey was lonely. His wife Gerd was off busy wrapping up her duties as the goddess of winter, so that he could get ready to bring summer to the worlds, especially Midgard.

So, he went back home, sat on his throne and tried to complete a few kingly and godly duties, but he grew bored of that as well. As he was reading, he dozed off for a while. Soon, his nap turned into deep sleep and while he was sleeping, he had one long terrible nightmare.

He dreamt that because he had gone to sleep for longer than he intended to, summer was late. Because summer was late, on Midgard, even though winter was over, nothing had begun to grow, or thaw. The skies were still gray, and because the weather was so strange, food was in short supply.

He dreamt that soon there was very little food and the humans were beginning to fight with each other. "Why doesn't Frey bring the summer?" one cried. "Perhaps we have displeased him!" cried another.

In their hunger and confusion, some evil people decided to convince a village that the only way to gain Frey's approval was to sacrifice nine people to him and to give him gold equal to that sacrifice, too. These evil people planned to then come back and steal the gold.

At this point his dreams became sharper and clearer, the way they do when you feel as though you're going to come awake at any moment.

As the villagers returned to their village to try and collect enough gold and choose who would be the nine sacrifices, they saw the priest's little son Saklauss (Sok-ley-si) sitting in the dirt by the temple playing with an idol of Frey. Saklauss thought it was a doll or an action figure, so he was playing with it and dragging it through the mud and having a grand time imagining adventures for the doll.

The villagers were outraged! "No wonder Frey had abandoned us," they yelled, "look at how this little boy insults him!" As they began to hit little Saklauss, he cried out loudly. He managed to escape into the forest, but he got lost. And in the dark and dangerous forest, wild animals killed him.

As soon as Frey heard the boy cry out, he woke up and went frantically to look at Midgard. He was horrified, because his nightmare had been a vision. Saklauss had been killed all because Frey had taken a nap.

However, Frey was going to set this right as soon as possible. He got on his magic boar Gullinbursti (Good-lin-push-teh), and sped to Helheim where Saklauss's soul would go. He and Gullinbursti raced through the worlds faster and faster until they were both just a blur of light and soon reached the dark world of Helheim. He looked at the long queue of people waiting outside the gate to get inside — there were millions of people. How would he ever find Saklauss?

Just then, he heard the sound of a child crying. It could have been any child, but Frey did not like seeing children cry, so he went to find them - and there he was. It was Saklauss after all. Frey got off his boar, went to Saklauss, and pulled him into a hug. The light and warmth from Frey calmed the boy and he hugged Frey back. As he opened his eyes, he felt something burrow under his arm. Gullinbursti had snuggled his nose under Saklauss's little arm and was comforting him, too.

Just then, Frey heard a tap-tap-tapping noise behind him and he turned. Saklauss gasped, and Frey just sighed. It was the goddess Hel tapping her foot.

"What do you think you're doing, Frey?" demanded Hel icily. She wasn't mad, she was just cold.

"I can explain," said Frey.

"Oh? Well, go on then." She raised her only eyebrow on the side of her face that had a face. Hel was half-skeleton plus half normal, which equaled a whole goddess. One side of her face and body was just bones, while the other side looked like a beautiful woman. Despite what she looked like, she was a kind, but stern, goddess.

"I took a nap, but the nap turned into a deep sleep of magic, and so I couldn't bring summer and because of that Saklauss got killed. Please let him go, Hel."

Hel looked at Frey as though he was crazy, before saying, "What? No, I got the second part," she interrupted him before he could start talking, holding up her hand. "Explain how this was your fault, and explain in detail." So, Frey explained in detail.

After he had finished, Hel looked at Saklauss in sympathy and then regretfully at Frey. "I'm sorry, Frey. I'd like to help, but he doesn't have a body to go back to. And while it is unfair that he died before he was supposed to, he won't be treated badly in my home, you know."

"I know, but I have a plan for that. Listen, I promise to buy his soul from you with gold, and then give him a new body. I'm just worried Odin might yell at you," Frey said.

"Odin can't tell me what to do," sniffed Hel. "Ignore him. And if you can find a body, this might work. And having all that gold warming my hall will make the people happy, too. You have a deal."

They shook hands with Frey promising to send the gold to Hel as soon as possible. Then he and Saklauss climbed on top of Gullinbursti and went to Saklauss's village in Midgard. There Frey asked him, "So, what kind of body would you like?"

Saklauss thought for a minute and answered, "I don't want to go back to the village because they were all mean to me. And even though the forest was where I got killed, I still love how beautiful it is. Can you give me a body that will let me live there without having to be afraid?"

Frey smiled at the smart boy and answered, "Yes, I'll turn you into a stag with such huge antlers that all the animals in the forest will be afraid of you and will leave you alone. Is that what you want?"

"Yes please, and thank you!" said the excited little boy. Frey sang a magic song known only to the Vanir gods, and where Saklauss had been standing, there now stood a bigger than big stag with massive, grand antlers on his head.

Satisfied that he had done all he could, Frey went home where Gerd was waiting for him and told her everything. She was happy the little boy was safe, but was a little worried too. "You made sure none of the other animals would be able to hurt him, but what about the humans and giants?"

"Hadn't thought of that, babe. What do you think I should do?" asked Frey. He loved it when Gerd got involved like this. He just loved Gerd, and didn't regret giving his sword away to win her love for an instant, even though he now had no weapon. She was always kind, caring, sensible, and had lots of wisdom to give.

"I think you should check up on him once in a while. Maybe have some kind of warning system for him just in case he gets in trouble."

"Good idea. But I think he should be okay," Frey said, crossing his fingers.

Unfortunately, Gerd was right. For a good number of years Saklauss the stag lived in peace, and neither human nor animal bothered him. But one day while Frey was out in the woods throwing truffles for Gullinbursti to eat, and making Gerd laugh, he heard Saklauss the stag cry out in his head.

Quickly he told Gerd, and called Gullinbursti to him so they could go see what was wrong. But he hesitated for a minute. "Gerd, Odin is supposed to come to Vanaheim today. He wants to grow grapes inside Valhalla and he wants to learn Vanir magic to do it."

"Don't worry about him. Odin's grapes can wait, and if they can't I'll cover for you. But you need to go. Now," She urged.

"You're the best, babe." He kissed her quickly and set off for Midgard.

When he reached the forest, he and the boar searched the woods swiftly. There in a small clearing was Saklauss the stag, alive but hurt badly. He had an arrow in his side, and was bleeding profusely. Worst of all, it seemed as though someone had hit him on the head as well, because his beautiful antlers were twisted and bleeding as well.

This time, instead of feeling guilty, Frey was angry. "Who did this to you Saklauss?"

The stag grunted softly at Frey.

"Beli (Bel-yah)? Who is Beli? And why would he do this?" asked Frey.

The stag grunted a few more times, telling Frey everything, and Frey grew angrier and angrier. "So, you're telling me Beli is a frost giant and he's hunting animals in Midgard because he finished hunting in his part of the forest in Jotunheim? How did he even get past the eyebrow wall?" The stag made a sound between a huff and a bleat.

"Ah. He tricked the humans into giving him a ride. Foolish humans," he said, irritated. Just then, both he and the stag heard footsteps stomping along to where they were. Frey told Saklauss, "I will heal you so you can run away, but since I don't have a weapon, this fight might take a while, so stay away from this part of the forest, alright?"

Saklauss looked at Frey with affection, grunted at him again and gently bowed his head before The Lord of Summer.

Frey gasped. "Are you sure?" he asked.

The stag bobbed its head.

"I would be honored, Saklauss. And once I'm done, I'll give you a new set." promised Frey. He placed his hand on the stag's head, whispered magic words, and lifted the antlers off Saklauss' head as easily as though he was removing a baseball hat. He finished healing the stag's wounds and told him to run and hide as the footsteps grew closer and closer.

Just as the stag had run away, Beli the frost giant shoved his way through the clearing. He didn't notice Frey at first since he was busy looking for the stag with the enormous antlers.

"Hey, where did the stag go? Here, staggy staggy!" He called.

Frey hated frost giants just as much as Thor did, but he didn't usually fight them. However, this time he was so mad, he wasn't going to let the giant get away scott-free.

"Hey!" yelled Frey. "Hey you. I'm talking to you, stinky!"

The giant looked up, then he looked around, and then finally he looked down. "Who are you calling 'stinky', you tiny torchlight?" he shouted. "Who are you anyway, and what did you do with my stag?"

"I set the stag free! My name is Frey, and you aren't just stinky. You're a stinky, rotten, poo-faced coward!"

"WHAT DID YOU CALL ME?" Beli roared.

"Oh, I'm sorry. I didn't realize you were deaf. I'll say it louder. YOU'RE A POO-FACED COWARD WHO WON'T PICK ON SOMEONE YOUR OWN SIZE!"

"You're hardly my size, puny. And besides, I've heard all about Frey the dumb god who gave away his sword for love," sneered Beli. "What are you going to fight me with? A love song? A cushion? A stick?"

"How about I fight you with this?" Frey said, and in one swift motion he pulled the antlers from behind him, and held it up high in one hand. As he held it up, the antlers began to glow with the ancient magic of the Vanir gods, and the heat and power of summer.

Frey leapt up and struck Beli under his jaw with the antlers. Beli staggered and swung wildly at Frey with his club, but Frey dodged the blow, ducked under his arm, and hit him again. Beli shook the blood and sweat out of his eyes and snarled at Frey, "You're dead, buddy. And once I kill you, I'm going to go find that stag and smash its head in, too."

This was a mistake. You can tell it was a mistake. I can tell it was a mistake. All the animals of the forest, and everyone else were able to tell this was a mistake. Except for Beli. Who decided the best way to deal with an angry god was to make him even more angry?

As Beli swung his club, Frey saw Saklauss's blood on the club from before. He was so angry that the heat of summer turned into a raging fire. He leapt straight at Beli, and swung his antlers at his head so hard that his head went flying off his shoulders in the opposite direction.

Then Frey calmed down and summer became normal again.

Everything was green, blooming, and lovely.

"Saklauss!" called Frey, and Saklauss trotted out of the thicket he had been hiding in. "Thank you for the gift of your antlers. They are a wonderful weapon, and I know I shall use them at Ragnarok to fight Surt."

The stag bleated at Frey, and Frey reassured him, "Oh no. Not for a long while. But let's not talk about that. Instead, here's what I can do. I can take you to a forest far away from humans or giants and you can stay there, or I can hide this forest so that humans and giants won't discover it for a thousand years. What would you like me to do?"

Saklauss grunted.

"Okay, option number two it is," Frey said. Then he stood back and sang a song of secrets and hiding. The forest blinked in and out of focus as though it was television switching itself on and off. "There you go," said Frey. "Live in safety and in happiness, little buddy. I'll visit when I can."

Then he climbed on to Gullinbursti, and set off towards Vanaheim to tell Gerd all about his adventure and show off his new weapon.

CHAPTER 9: NINE MOTHERS FOR HEIMDALL

I'm sure you know plenty of people who have two moms, or two dads, and that makes sense. But have you ever heard of someone who had *nine* moms? You and I know that moms are loving but scary people at the best of times, now imagine having nine! If you can't, well, let's read and imagine it together.

HALF RIG, HALF HEIMDALL

We've heard about so many of the gods already. Did you know that while Njord is the god of sea and the winds, there is another god who is the god of the sea and the waves? This god's name is Aegir (Ey-yir). He and his wife Ran (Rah-nh) live under the sea in a huge hidden castle.

Now, they don't really have mermaids in the castle. Instead, they have ghosts. Do you remember how we read about Hel being a place for normal dead people? In the same way, Aegir and Ran's underwater kingdom was home to all the souls of people who had drowned in the sea.

Aegir and Ran also had nine daughters. They were as beautiful as the ocean on a sunny beach day, and as dangerous as a tsunami. A tsunami is what you call a tidal wave so big and wide it looks as though it is touching the sky and can destroy entire islands in one go.

That is how dangerous Aegir and Ran's daughters were when they were angry. For the most part, they liked to talk with their ghost friends, explore the sea, and sometimes go exploring the land. Their names were Kolga (Kool-gah), Duva (Doo-vah), Blodughadda (Blow-do-gat-ha), Bara (Bow-rah), Bylgja (Bilg-yah), Hronn (Hrun), Hevring (Hevh-ring), Unnur (Oon-nur), and Himinglava (He-ming-lavuh), and they were super protective of each other.

Once, during a trip to Vanaheim, Odin met one of the sisters and they fell in love and had a baby. But Odin had to go back to Asgard, and she couldn't go with him. So, they parted sadly and promised to be there if ever one of them needed the other.

Now, no one knows which sister had the baby, because they knew their dad and mum would be angry because they didn't like Odin very much and would have blamed him. So, all nine sisters hid in the deepest, darkest part of the ocean — it was even deeper and darker than the Marianas Trench. There they stayed and promised each other that they would never tell which one of them had the baby, and the baby would instead be known as the child with nine mothers.

When Aegir and Ran eventually found out, because one: it is impossible to hide a baby, and two: it is impossible to hide stuff from your mum and dad, they were mad. But no matter how much they yelled and threatened to ground them forever and ever, not one single sister tattled. My sibling tattles on me if I take half an extra helping of dessert. Is your sibling like mine, or are they more like the nine sisters?

On with the story.

The sisters wanted to keep the baby, but they knew he would have a better chance of surviving with Odin. So, they put him on a little boat and called Odin to come pick him up from the boat. Odin came immediately, and was so happy with the way the baby grabbed his finger, that he promised to take the baby to Asgard immediately.

When Frigg saw Odin coming home with the baby, she went straight up to him and smacked him on his head. Odin, I mean; not the baby.

"Ow!" said Odin, "What was that for?"

"You're carrying the baby all wrong!" she snapped at him. "Just because he's a demi-god, doesn't mean you can dangle him like a noodle. Give me the baby," she said, snatching him out of Odin's arms. "Isn't that right, darling? You're not a noodle, are you, precious?" she cooed at the baby. The baby cooed back at her. Frigg was so delighted and loved the child so much, that she named him Heimdall and then glared at Odin, daring him to disagree with her name choice.

"I think it's a wonderful name, Frigg, but uh, it's a very godly name, isn't it?" he said cautiously.

"In case you hadn't noticed, he *is* a god, Odin." Frigg rolled her eyes.

"Only half," muttered Odin.

"What was that?" asked Frigg sharply.

"I said I forgot my staff," said Odin loudly.

"Hmph," Frigg said and went inside. After a couple of days, Odin came to the nursery where Njord, Skadi, and Frigg were sitting and playing with Heimdall. Skadi was making flurries of snow above his crib, while Njord made the winds blow the snow around.

Odin waggled his head at Frigg who understood he wanted to talk to her privately, so she followed him out into the hallway. "Yes dear, what's on your mind?" she asked.

"I did a bit of seidr magic, the way you taught me, about Heimdall," he confessed nervously. Frigg just smiled serenely and said, "I wondered when you would try to see his future. I did it the day he arrived!" she snickered. But then she grew serious. "I know sending him to Midgard is the right thing to do, but Odin, it'll be so long till we see him again!"

"I know, but he has a human life and destiny that he has to fulfil, Frigg. Besides, we're gods! Time isn't a big deal for us, remember?" he reminded her.

"I know, but I'll miss him," she said sadly.

Odin had looked in Heimdall's future and seen that he must live as a human before he could become a god. The humans needed a hero anyway, so Heimdall would first become a hero and complete his duties on earth, and then become a god.

Odin took him to Midgard and left him near a fisherman's house. The fisherman found the child crying, so he took him inside and cared for him. He named the baby Rig (Ree-hg), and

Heimdall grew up on Midgard as Rig. Unlike his fisherman-dad, Rig was a little wary of the water, because he always felt as though the sea was watching him. He didn't know he was right, since all of his nine mothers would watch him from afar just to see how he was.

Rig grew up fast, and as a fisherman's son, he grew up to be patient, strong, brave, humble, and true. He also grew up to be very handsome, and many women wanted to marry him. Once he was old enough, he went away to fight in wars, and fight dragons and all kinds of monsters — even the human kind of monsters.

Soon, because of all the battles and adventures, the Norse people admired and loved Rig so much, they made him King. Everyone always had plenty to eat, fights were settled calmly and fairly, and everyone was happy. Odin, Frigg, and his nine mothers who were always watching from afar, were very proud of him.

But even though he was a demi-god — something he didn't know yet — the human half of him grew old, and died. Everyone was standing around and crying and sobbing, when a whopping great flock of birds flew down and fluttered around his body. Then, the birds put him on their back and flew him all the way up to Asgard.

There, Odin sang his rune song over him, and Rig woke up. He looked around and saw Odin and Frigg standing there waiting to welcome him. He got slowly out of the bed the birds had placed him in and noticed that the way his bones used to creak and hurt when he was old had all disappeared. He looked at himself and was astounded — which means he was shocked in a good way — to see he was young and strong again!

Odin and Frigg explained all that had happened and told him that the human half of him had to die, before he could live properly as one of the Aesir gods. They told him his godly name was Heimdall, and that he would be the guardian god of Asgard.

Then they told him about his nine mothers, and he decided

to go visit them on the shores of Vanaheim before taking up his godly duties. And that is how Heimdall is the god with nine mothers (Arithharger, 2013).

CHAPTER 10: THE END, OR IS IT?

W ell, here we are. We're at the end. Or are we? We're almost at the end, but there's still a little more. So, let's go. Together.

THE END IS THE BEGINNING IS THE END

The end doesn't always have to be a sad thing. Have you seen a lotus flower? It grows once a year in swampy places. The roots reach deep down into the mud, while the leaves float on top and then, slowly the flower unfurls. One petal at a time. Despite the dirty surroundings, the flower stays clean and beautiful. Once it has finished blooming, it closes its petals, folds up on itself and sinks into the water. It seems sad that such a beautiful thing could have such a fleeting life.

But underneath, there is magic. The seed hidden inside the lotus sinks into the mud, and there, it waits to grow again. That is what endings and beginnings are like, like an echo which ends where it starts – at the opening of a cave. Or like a story which finds another story like itself and ends and begins at the same time.

Do you remember how we read about King Arthur? When Arthur died, the legends say he was taken away to rest in the land of Avalon, until Great Britain needs him again.

This is similar to what happens in the story of Sigmund. King Volsung (Fol-zong), Sigmund's (Seeg-mond) father, built a beautiful palace built with a large tree growing in the center of the throne room. The tree, which was named Barnstock, stretched through the roof and out into the open.

One evening when King Volsung had given a party to celebrate King Siggeir (Si-gah) and his daughter Princess Signy's (Sig-nee) engagement, an old one-eyed stranger came into the hall wearing a hood. He stood in front of the tree, drew a sword and plunged it down right to the hilt into the trunk, saying, "Whomever can pull the sword from the tree, shall keep it and always find victory." And the old man, who was Odin in disguise, disappeared.

All the people present there tried to pull the sword from the tree, including King Volsung and King Siggeir, all without success. Then Sigmund came forward, put his hand on the hilt, and pulled the sword from the trunk as easily as though he were drawing it out of butter.

Everyone congratulated Sigmund, but Siggeir was full of envy, and offered to buy the sword in exchange for gold.

Sigmund refused, saying, "The will of the gods sent this sword to my hands and I will not give it away."

With the sword, Sigmund became a great warrior and a mighty king, until he was betrayed. When he was betrayed, he mistakenly did something which caused Odin's favor to be taken away from him, and he died. But, some legends say he and his wife sleep in a cave, while others say it is his son who sleeps, only to wake again when he will be needed in battle with his trusty sword Gram by his side.

Perhaps some parts of these myths were true. Perhaps there was a king who was that amazing. Perhaps there was a sword so sharp it could cut through a solid block of iron (Sigmund, n.d.).

Perhaps, you will read The Volsunga Saga and realize it meant something else entirely!

CONCLUSION

(Or the part everyone reads in the hope there is one last story left).

We've read all about endings and beginnings, so you know that even though we've reached the end of the book, the stories you will read or imagine are just beginning.

So, let me leave you with one last story which will take you right back to the start. The story of Ragnarok — which isn't as sad as it sounds.

It will begin with wars in every single country on earth. Heimdall will blow the horn and all the gods and warriors will then ride into battle against the frost giants, monsters, and Loki, who is now completely evil.

Odin will be killed by Fenris (Fen-rhis), the wolf who will break free of his chains, but his son Vidar (Vee-dar) will kill Fenris. Thor will fight the giant snake, and it will be his greatest battle. He will kill the snake, but the snake poison will allow him to take only nine steps, before he falls down dead. Heimdall will fight Loki, and they will kill each other.

Frey will fight Surt, the fire giant of Muspel. If he had his sword, he would have survived, but he would still manage to wound Surt a little, before he himself is killed. Then Surt will use the fires of Muspel to burn everything and everyone, and he will die as well.

But then, once the fires have burned down, water will wash over the world, and a new world will rise up out of it, with sparkling rivers, evergreen forests, a blue sea, a bright sun in a clear sky, and fields upon fields of flowers. And two people, a man and a woman, will walk through those fields. They are the two people The World Tree hid in its trunk and kept safe.

And on another branch, Asgard and Vanaheim will rise out of the smoke and fire, more beautiful than ever before. Thor's sons Magni (Mak-nih) and Modi (Moody), Vidar and Vali (Va-lih), the sons of Odin, Hel, Baldr, and other gods and goddesses stroll through the worlds, talking, laughing and making everything seem bright (Wikipedia Contributors, 2020).

"But I thought you said it wouldn't be as sad as it sounds!" you cry. My dear confused friends, I promise you an ending is not a sad thing at all. It makes way for something new - a new plan, a new song, a new painting, a new job, a new life... and even, a new story.

Write your own stories. Write your own version of the myths. Maybe you read a myth and something deep inside you said this was not how it happened, and you decide to take parts of that story and make something new of it the way I did with Frey's story of the antlers (How Frey Gained the Antlers of Saklauss | Thomas Hewitt's Poetry, n.d.)!

Start somewhere. But if you can't decide where to start, start at the end. I know that sounds strange, but a poet named T.S Eliot (1971, p. 21) once wrote a poem called, "Little Gilding". The poem says *"What we call the beginning is often the end / And to make an end is to make a beginning. / The end is where we start from."*

We may have come to the end of this book, but you now have the chance to read (or create!) something new. No ending is truly final or forever. So, enjoy the end, and celebrate the promise of a new story.

Good luck!

FREE BONUS FROM HBA: EBOOK BUNDLE

Greetings!

First of all, thank you for reading our books. As fellow passionate readers of history and mythology we aim to create the very best books for our readers.

Now, we invite you to join our VIP list. As a welcome gift we offer the History & Mythology Ebook Bundle below for free. Plus you can be the first to receive new books and exclusives! Remember it's 100% free to join.

Simply click the link below to join.

Click Here For Your Free Bonus
(https://www.subscribepage.com/hba)

Keep upto date with us on:

YouTube: History Brought Alive

Facebook: History Brought Alive

www.historybroughtalive.com

REFERENCES

Alectryon (mythology). (2021, April 29). Wikipedia. https://en.wikipedia.org/wiki/Alectryon_(mythology)

Álfheimr. (2021). Religion Wiki. https://religion.wikia.org/wiki/%C3%81lfheimr

Arithharger. (2013, October 7). *Heimdall's Birth*. Whispers of Yggdrasi https://arithharger.wordpress.com/2013/10/07/heimdalls-birth/

B, V. (2018). Man holding rope. In *https://unsplash.com/photos/IYyvakvhi7I*.

Branstock. (n.d.). Britannica Kids. Retrieved August 15, 2021, from https://kids.britannica.com/students/article/Branstock/310360

Cartwright, M. (2015, May 16). *Brahma*. World History Encyclopedia. https://www.worldhistory.org/Brahma/

Chidanand, A. (2017). Ocean moody waves. In *Image by Aadya Chidanand from Pixabay*.

Climo, S., & Florczak, R. (2001). *The Persian Cinderella*. Harpercollins.

Climo, S., & Heller, R. (1992). *The Egyptian Cinderella*. Harpertrophy.

Eliot, T. S. (1971). *Four quartets*. Mariner Books, Houghton Mifflin Harcourt, [201.

Furman, P. (2016). Person wearing red and white coat. In *Photo by Paweł Furman on Unsplash*.

Girls, G. (2020). Reindeer Elk. In *Image by GypsyGirlS from Pixabay*.

Hel (The Underworld) - Norse Mythology for Smart People. (2012). Norse Mythology for Smart People. https://norse-mythology.org/cosmology/the-nine-worlds/helheim/

How Frey Gained the Antlers of Saklauss | Thomas Hewitt's Poetry. (n.d.). Thomashewitt.org. Retrieved August 28, 2021, from https://thomashewitt.org/how-frey-gained-the-antlers-of-saklauss/

Hrustall. (2021). Дмитрий Хрусталев-Григорьев. In *Photo by Дмитрий Хрусталев-Григорьев on Unsplash.*

Keller, S. (2017). Fantasy landscape cave. In *Image by Stefan Keller from Pixabay.*

Krause, W. (2010). Fantasy world. In *Image by Willgard Krause from Pixabay.*

Nilsson, O. (2017). Wind in the grey mane. In *Photo by Oscar Nilsson on Unsplash.*

NORSE GODS: MÁNI – Ýdalir. (2018). Ydalir.ca. http://ydalir.ca/norsegods/mani/

NORSE GODS: SÓL – Ýdalir. (n.d.). Ydalir.ca. http://ydalir.ca/norsegods/sol/

Northern Norway – where the sun never sets. (n.d.). Www.visitnorway.com. https://www.visitnorway.com/things-to-do/nature-attractions/midnight-sun/

Ragnarok | Encyclopedia.com. (2019). Encyclopedia.com. https://www.encyclopedia.com/literature-and-arts/classical-literature-mythology-and-folklore/folklore-and-mythology/ragnarok

Recap. (n.d.). Dictionary.cambridge.org. Retrieved August 20, 2021, from https://dictionary.cambridge.org/dictionary/english/recap

San, R. D. (1997). *Sootface : an Ojibwa Cinderella tale.* Bantam Doubleday Books For Young Readers.

Sigmund. (n.d.). Britannica Kids. Retrieved August 28, 2021, from https://kids.britannica.com/students/article/Sigmund/313536

Skjalden. (2018, July 30). *The Mead of Poetry - Nordic Culture - Norse mythology.* Nordic Culture. https://skjalden.com/mead-of-poetry/

Skjalden. (2020, September 19). *Yggdrasil - The World Tree - Norse Mythology.* Nordic Culture. https://skjalden.com/yggdrasil/

Skjalden. (2017, September 24). *Thor's Duel with Hrungnir - Norse Sagas - Norse Mythology.* Nordic Culture. https://skjalden.com/giant-hrungnir/

Skov Andersen, J. (2015, May 6). *Fashionable Vikings loved colours, fur, and silk.* Sciencenordic.com. https://sciencenordic.com/archaeology-history-denmark-society--culture/fashionable-vikings-loved-colours-fur-and-silk/1417589

Staff, History. com. (2018, August 29). *Was King Arthur a real person?* HISTORY. https://www.history.com/news/was-king-arthur-a-real-person

Stavrou, D., & Tchetchik, D. (2017, December 18). *In extraordinary photos: Sweden says a long goodbye to sunlight.* Haaretz.com. https://www.haaretz.com/world-news/MAGAZINE-in-extraordinary-photos-the-swedes-say-a-long-goodbye-to-sunlight-1.5628672

Survival International. (2018). *Sentinelese.* Survivalinternational.org. https://www.survivalinternational.org/tribes/sentinelese

Tanis, L. (2017). Pandora The World of Avatar. In *Photo by Luke Tanis on Unsplash.*

White, T. H., & Shadbolt, R. (1998). *The sword in the stone.* Harpercollins Children's Books.

Wikipedia Contributors. (2019, October 23). *Edda.* Wikipedia; Wikimedia Foundation. https://en.wikipedia.org/wiki/Edda

Wikipedia Contributors. (2020, January 9). *Ragnarök*. Wikipedia; Wikimedia Foundation. https://en.wikipedia.org/wiki/Ragnar%C3%B6k

Yantis, M. (2021). blue and brown ceramic vase. In *Photo by Michael Yantis on Unsplash*.

Zak, P. (2013, December 17). *How Stories Change the Brain*. Greater Good. https://greatergood.berkeley.edu/article/item/how_stories_change_brain

Printed in Great Britain
by Amazon